Convert It

by

Michael P. Brown

with

Shari Prange

A Step-By-Step Manual
For Converting
An Internal Combustion Vehicle
To Electric Power

Published by
Future Books, an imprint of
South Florida Electric Auto Association
1402 East Los Olas Boulevard
Ft. Lauderdale, FL   33301

Printed in the United States.

Printing history:
    First edition published in the United States by Electro Automotive, 1989
    Second edition published in the United States by Electro Automotive, 1990
    Third edition published in the United States by Future Books, an imprint of the South Florida Electric Auto Association, 1993

NOTICE: Every effort has been taken to insure that the information in this book is accurate and complete as of the date of printing. Authors and publishers cannot accept any liability for loss, damage, or injury incurred in connection with the use of this information, or resulting from any errors in or omissions from the information given.

Publisher's Cataloging in Publication
(Prepared by Quality Books Inc.)

Brown, Michael P.
    Convert it : a step-by-step manual for converting an internal combustion vehicle to electric power / Michael P. Brown.
    p. cm.
    Includes index.
    ISBN 1-879857-94-4

1. Automobiles, Electric. I. Title.

TL220.B76 1993   629.250'2
                                       QBI93-1262

CONTENTS

ACKNOWLEDGEMENTS

I would like to thank (in alphabetical order) the following people who have provided technical information, proofreading, illustrations, and moral support for this project: Herb Adams, John Anderson, Larry Burriesci, D. Clarke, Scott Cornell, Eric Dieroff, Ruth MacDougall, Paul McCain, Bob McKee, Steve Pombo, Steve Post, Rich Prange, and Damian Taylor.

Special thanks to N. Jell for making this third edition possible.

PHOTOGRAPHS

All photographs were taken by Shari Prange, unless otherwise credited, and are individually the property of their respective contributors. The cover photo shows author Michael Brown in Santa Cruz, California, with two of his electric cars. In the foreground is a 1965 Fiberfab Aztec I body on a VW Bug chassis. In the background is the 1981 VW Rabbit conversion prototype for the Voltsrabbit™ kit.

FOR A CATALOG OF ELECTRIC VEHICLE COMPONENTS:

Send $5.00 (postage & sales tax included) to:
> Electro Automotive
> P. O. Box 1113-CI
> Felton, CA 95018

Catalog also lists other electric vehicle books and videos for sale.

Outside the United States and Canada, please send $10.00. U.S. dollars only.

TO ORDER COPIES OF THIS BOOK:

Send $24.95, plus $3.50 U.S. postage or $8.50 foreign postage, to above address. In California, add sales tax. U.S. dollars only.

1

Introduction

So you'd like to build an electric car. You're not quite sure where to start, and that's why you're holding this book. You've come to the right place.

You don't have to be a professional mechanic to use this book or build your car. In fact, this manual was written for the hobbyist or student. We'll start out talking a little bit about what you can expect from an electric car, just to be sure that the finished reality will match your hopes. We'll talk about how to choose a car to convert, and about how to strip it to make the conversion easy. We'll go step by step through installing each component, and talk a little bit about why we chose the component we did, and why we installed it the way we did. At the end, we'll test the system, and talk about charging, driving techniques, and suggested maintenance.

It doesn't matter whether your car starts life as a gas or diesel car, front or rear drive, or even a pickup truck or kit car. We'll address all of those variations along the way.

We're going to be spending quite a bit of time together for the next hundred or so pages, so we should get to know each other a little first.

I already know you. You're intrigued by things that are a little out of the ordinary or ahead of their time. You find a kind of beauty in systems that are clean, efficient, and simple. The proper engineering term is 'elegant'. You're concerned about increasing pollution, and the increasing complexity of the internal combustion engine. And you're excited by the idea of driving an unusual car that you built yourself.

Author Michael Brown

It's only fair that you know a little about me, and my automotive background. First, I'm a car person, and have been all my life. I've been a professional mechanic for twenty-eight years, and built some race cars along the way. My experience with cars has been *very* hands-on, not theoretical, and this has given me a healthy respect for the ways things can go wrong.

Having my own shop for seventeen years also taught me about drivers. I learned what people expect from their cars, and how they are likely to neglect them, misuse them, or be confused and intimidated by them. I believe the interaction between the car and driver is as important as the internal workings of the machine.

In 1979, during the second gas crisis, one of my customers asked me to build an electric car for him. I had just quit racing, and was ripe for an interesting project. As the owner of a gas station, I could see a promising future for electrics.

I built the car, which was a VW Bug chassis with a Fiberfab Aztec body, and learned a lot in the process. One of the things I

"Build cars today
with parts that are
reliably available
today."

learned was that there were no good sources for parts. There were scattered suppliers, many of them unreliable. Most people were building cars with scavenged surplus parts from aircraft and homebrew concoctions that were often frightening.

By the time the car was finished, Electro Automotive was born: a conversion parts supply business. I spent several years researching available production components and seeking out manufacturers who would build to our specifications. It was a very educational experience.

Over the years, I have built more than a dozen electric cars, and have supplied parts and advice for more than a hundred projects. Every car taught me something, and these little bits of knowledge gradually accumulated into a few basic principles that express my personal philosophy on electric cars. These are the principles on which this manual is based.

Simplicity. Complexity means opportunities for failure. The simpler a system is, the less there is to go wrong. KISS——Keep It Simple, Stupid.

Ease of use. Simplicity of design must be matched by simplicity of operation. An electric car should be familiar and non-threatening, even to a novice driver. Just as mechanical complications lead to mechanical failures, complicated operating procedures lead to human failures.

Proven reliability. I don't want promises or computer projections——I want an actual track record. People depend heavily on their cars. If the car isn't reliable, it's worthless. Experimental technologies may be great boons to electric cars someday, but the place to test them is not in a car someone depends on to get to work.

This is also a reason not to re-invent the wheel. Automotive manufacturers put millions of engineering design hours into their vehicles. It makes sense to use as much of their design as possible, and make our own modifications as compatible as possible with the original car.

Safety. For every component and system, ask the question, "What would happen if this failed?" Safety generally means isolation: isolating the electricity to a specific path, quickly isolating a failed component from the rest of the system, and isolating potentially dangerous components from the passengers.

Availability. Build cars today with parts that are reliably available today. Not yesterday's out-of-production leftovers, and not tomorrow's pre-production test samples.

Affordability. There are some wonderful technologies that are in production and readily available, and have been proven to offer impressive performance. However, if they cost five times the value of the rest of the car, what's the point?

The final result of following these principles will be an electric car that is practical and pleasant to drive for the average person in normal daily use.

Now let's figure out how an electric car might fit into your life.

2

"An EV is a
mission-intensive car.
It should not be
expected to be
all things
to all people."

Facts About Electric Vehicles

The workings of an electric vehicle (EV) are very simple. Electricity moves from the power source, which is probably a wall socket, through a charger, and into the battery pack. When the ignition key is turned, the main contactor closes, allowing electricity to move from the batteries to the speed controller. As the throttle is depressed, the potbox sends a signal to the controller telling it how much electricity to release to the motor. The speed of the motor varies depending on how much electricity it gets. The motor is connected to the transmission by an adaptor plate. The power goes from the motor, through the transmission, and out to the wheels as in a gas car. That's it in a nutshell. We'll talk about each of these parts in more detail later.

Before you build an EV for yourself, compare the performance of a typical EV with your intended uses for it, and make sure the two are compatible. An EV is a mission-intensive car. It should not be expected to be all things to all people. A sports car is not expected to carry lots of kids, and a luxury car is not expected to be especially economical or suited to off-road driving. Likewise, an EV has its own niche.

An EV is like a microwave oven. There are a lot of things a microwave can't do, such as brown food, bake an angel food cake, cook in metal pans, or prepare an entire Thanksgiving dinner. A conventional oven can do all those things. Yet the limitations of microwave ovens haven't dampened their sales or popularity. Nor have microwaves replaced conventional ovens, and no one is expecting them to do so. What a microwave does, it does very well. So it is with an EV.

At the current state of the technology, there are two applications into which EVs fit admirably.

Commuter Car. Most American households have more than one car, and often one of them is used almost entirely for commuting or local errand-running. In fact, the average miles per day per vehicle in this country is less than thirty. An EV is ideal for this type of use.

Some people think of an EV as a second car, and that's fine, but it depends on how you define 'first' and 'second'. Our gas car gets more mileage than the electric, but that's because we use it for long distance driving. The EV gets used more often, but for shorter trips. We think of our EV as our first car, because it's our first choice.

Fun Car. An EV is a fun project to build, and will give you the satisfaction of creating something that is uniquely yours. It's fun to drive, and if you have graphics on it to identify it as electric, it will introduce you to a lot of friendly people at stoplights and in parking lots.

There are myriad events for electric cars, ranging from local parades and energy fairs, shows and road rallies, on up to closed course races. If you choose, you can be busy almost every weekend, collecting ribbons and trophies, meeting people who are fascinated by your car, and just having fun.

Your car can be demure and practical, or flashy and futuristic. The choice is yours.

What's An Electric Car Like?

Passenger/Cargo Room. This depends on the car you choose for conversion, and on your design. A car that starts out as a two-seat sports car will probably end up as a two-seat high-performance electric with little or no cargo space. At the other extreme, a converted four-door sedan or a small truck can provide quite reasonable performance while maintaining full passenger room, and most or all of the original cargo space.

This high-performance electric sports car (a converted 914 Porsche) has a top speed of 90 mph and a range of over 120 miles on a single charge.

Speed. Most modern EVs can do highway speeds of 50 - 60 mph. A car that is very heavy before conversion will do less well. A very light car such as a kit car, or a very aerodynamic sports car, may have a top speed of 80 - 90 mph. Acceleration is good, and is directly related to the weight of the car and the quality of the components used.

Horsepower. It is difficult to compare electric motors to gas engines because their horsepower is rated differently. Gas engines are generally rated on dynos rather than in cars, with no load on them, not even things like alternator belts. They are rated at their peak horsepower. Electric motors, on the other hand, tend to be rated under load, and at their continuous duty rpm. A typical EV motor will have a continuous rating of 10 - 20 hp, which is all most cars need for cruising. It will have a peak rating of around 60 - 70 hp.

Range. The typical modern conversion should have a range of 60 - 80 miles in normal driving. This means some freeway, but largely stop-and-go surface streets with speeds of 30 - 40 mph. Higher-performance cars will get 100 miles or more. Range will decrease with weight, hills, or excessive stop-and-go traffic. There are many things that can be done (to the car, and to the driver's driving style) to improve range. We'll talk about these in more detail later.

There are two common questions that come up about range. The first is, "What happens when I run out of electricity?" You should be familiar with your car and its range, and you should have a gauge to give you a continuous reading on your state of charge, so dead batteries will not suddenly sneak up on you. Also, an electric car does not quit abruptly like a gas car. Instead, in the bottom 20% or so of its charge, performance will begin to fade gradually.

If you misjudge and reach the point where the car is moving too slowly to be safe in traffic, pull over and park for a few minutes. The batteries will 'grow amps' and recover some of their charge simply by resting. In five or ten minutes, you can drive on again. If necessary, you can do this several times over several miles until you get home, although it's not recommended as regular practice. However, just try to park an empty gas car and 'grow gas'!

Range Extenders. The second question is, "What if I want to take a trip? Can I put some kind of range extender on the car?" The most common strategy uses an internal combustion engine, and the car is called a hybrid. There are two types of hybrids. In a series hybrid, a generator is used to provide electricity for the motor, through a battery pack which acts as a storage buffer. In a parallel hybrid, the engine is actually an optional or auxiliary drive system for the car.

I have been personally involved in the building of both types, and found them both to be unsatisfactory for several reasons. For one thing, the hybrid concept violates the principle of simplicity. Everything in the internal combustion system and in the interface between the systems is a potential problem. Also, this reintroduces all the pollution, maintenance, and expense we had eliminated by converting to electric. One has to ask, "Is this hybrid any cleaner than the original internal combustion system?" It might actually be dirtier. Also, is the gas mileage any better?

An electric car requires approximately 10 kw of energy just to maintain cruising speed. Electricity comes in two types: AC and DC. Alternating current (AC) is household electricity. Its name comes from the fact that the flow of the current regularly reverses its direction. Direct current (DC) is battery current, and it flows in one direction only. Since generators are designed to put out AC current, this must be altered through a rectifier to DC to go into the batteries. Take a look at the size and price of a generator that can produce 10 kw DC.

Hybrid systems are also bulky, noisy, and expensive. In my opinion, they contradict everything an electric car is supposed to be, and to little advantage. If you have to go farther than the EV will take you, skip the complicated compromise and just drive a gas car.

Another suggested range extender is a solar panel. This can certainly be used, but the trade-offs will not be acceptable to most people. If you mount enough panels to cover the entire roof of the car, and if the car sits in the full sun all day long, the panels will only supply about 5 miles more range. If you live in a sunny climate

"Just try to park an empty gasoline car and 'grow gas'!"

and don't drive much, perhaps this could meet a large percentage of your needs. The continuous low level charge will help extend the overall life of your batteries. However, the panel is heavy, unaerodynamic, vulnerable to damage, and costs about $3,000.

This situation will not improve much, even though solar panels are improving in efficiency. If the solar panels were 100% efficient, instead of about 10%, it would still take an array 10' x 10' to supply enough power to charge a car solely from the panels.

The appropriate place for solar technology in relation to electric cars is at charging stations. Panels covering the roofs of parking areas, with receptacles at each stall, could provide some charge for working people while their cars sit idle all day.

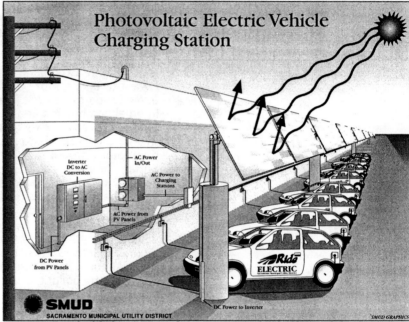

A solar charging station at the Sacramento Municipal Utility District. (Graphic courtesy of SMUD.)

A third suggested range extender is the quick-charge station. This may become a reality, but it isn't here yet. One problem is that quick charging requires massive amounts of current, and demand would probably coincide with other peak demands for power during the day. Another problem is that batteries can be damaged internally unless the charge is delivered in a carefully controlled manner.

A fourth suggested range extender is the exchange battery pack. This has been used with some success in purpose-built race cars, but has problems for ordinary conversions. For one thing, the typical battery pack weighs 1,000 pounds or more. It will require specialized equipment to handle this effectively. Also, in almost any car except a pickup truck, the batteries are not in one easy-to-reach module, but are in two or three separate packages in places where it's impossible to get a hoist or forklift. For the private individual, swapping battery packs means the added expense of a second pack. For battery swaps in a service station situation, all models of cars would have to use identical battery configurations—an impossibility with conversions, and highly unlikely even with ground-up designs.

"The best range extender for an electric car is a rental car."

A final suggested range extender is regenerative braking. In regenerative braking, the braking action of the car is used to generate electricity to charge the batteries. Usually the drive motor is used as the generator, but sometimes an automotive alternator is used.

Regeneration is tricky in a DC system. Special wiring is required for both the motor and controller. With improper installation, possible failures could include unintended acceleration instead of braking, or even damage to the motor. At this time, regenerative braking for the hobbyist conversion violates the simplicity and safety principles. This could change if a regen system were developed by a major controller manufacturer.

There is also some doubt about the value of regeneration. While it can be done effectively in an AC system (which is more expensive), in a DC system it may not actually provide enough charge to be worthwhile. The ideal regen condition is a long downhill. However, for many people their downhill stretch is when they first leave home, and the batteries are fully charged. In this instance, regen is useless.

In a typical conversion without regen, the motor freewheels and offers no resistance on a downhill. I live in the mountains, and my driving style includes using my downhill momentum to 'slingshot' up the next hill. If I had regen, I would be charging the batteries on the downhill, but the regen would also be slowing the car and reducing my momentum. I would have more charge going up the next hill, but less momentum. I suspect the loss of momentum would cancel out any charge gained.

Beyond this, range extension ideas start to include windmills on the roof, perpetual motion machines, and other schemes that are unworkable because they violate several laws of physics.

Let's get back to the original question of what to do about a long trip. First, how often do you drive farther than the electric car can go? Second, do you have a gas car available for those trips? If not, then the best range extender for an electric car, in my opinion, is a rental car.

Recharging. If your battery pack is drawn down completely, it will take ten to twelve hours to recharge using a 110-volt charger. This can be reduced to 6 - 8 hours with a 220-volt charger. When we get to the section on chargers, we'll talk more about the pros and cons of each. Development is underway on the concept of 'pulsing' chargers that can charge batteries much faster without damaging them.

Number of Batteries. Most conversions use 6-volt lead-acid golf car batteries. (We'll discuss different types of batteries later.) In general, pack voltage determines speed. A 72-volt system (twelve batteries) is the minimum, just barely acceptable for a road-going vehicle. This is only acceptable in a very light car that is never intended for freeway use. It will have performance similar to the original 1200 CC VW Bugs.

Most conversions use sixteen batteries, for a total pack voltage of 96 volts. For higher performance, heavy cars, or work vehicles such as light pickup trucks, a 120-volt system with twenty batteries is recommended.

EVs Don't Need:

Gasoline

Oil Change

Tune-up

Spark Plugs

Cap & Rotor

Valve Adjust

Air Filter

Oil Filter

Fuel Filter

Carburetor

Fuel Injectors

Distributor

Plug Wires

Fan Belt

Timing Belt

Water Pump

Radiator

Starter

Alternator

Hoses

Fuel Pump

Choke

Head Gasket

Valve Grind

Rings

Engine Overhaul

Manifold

Muffler

Catalytic Convertor

Smog Certificate

Cost & Time for Conversion. Costs will vary, depending on how complete and pre-fabricated your kit is, and how high-tech you want to get. At the low end, an acceptable conversion can be done for about $5,500 in parts and materials. This assumes that you will be designing and building your battery racks, battery boxes, and other mounts and brackets yourself, using the least expensive materials that are strong enough for the job.

On the high end, you can buy a completely pre-fabbed bolt-in kit and do your conversion for about $8,000, including such niceties as corrosion-resistant non-conductive powder-painted battery racks and welded polypropylene battery boxes.

In the stratospheric range, you can spend up to $50,000 in the blink of an eye on AC drive systems and exotic batteries, but the end product won't be substantially better for daily driving.

The above costs include batteries, but not the donor car, or any mechanical or aesthetic work needed.

Excluding exotic components, the cost of the kit varies inversely with the amount of time and effort needed to install it. The low-end kit will require 200 hours or more of your time, most of it design time. The high end pre-fabbed kit will require no design, fabrication, or welding, and can be installed in less than 40 hours if you're moderately handy with tools.

Operating Costs. Fuel (electricity) costs vary in each locale, but generally work out to about 2.5¢ - 5¢ per mile. This is about the same as fuel costs for a fuel-efficient gas car. Typical conversions use about .4 kwh/mile, so you can multiply that by your local rate. Some utilities offer special low rates for night-time off-peak charging of electric cars.

The real savings in an electric car comes from maintenance. There is a very long list of parts and services that electric cars don't need, and a very short list of parts and services they do need. Over the lifespan of the car, *even after factoring in periodic battery pack replacement,* the operating costs for an EV are only about 1/3 of those for a gas car. For example, on the newer cars the 30,000 mile services *alone* cost $300 - $500. This service comes up every 2 - 3 years, and is required to maintain the warranty.

It is harder to express the other area of savings in dollars. This is the time you save *not* stopping at the gas station, *not* getting the oil changed, *not* getting a tune-up, *not* arranging for a friend to help you drop off and pick up your car at the shop, etc.

Reliability. The EV, when properly built, is very reliable because it has so many fewer parts to fail. Most of the components are solid-state electronics with no moving parts.

Longevity. An electric car has a virtually infinite lifespan. The components will probably outlast the chassis. The batteries need to be replaced about every three to four years. The motor brushes need to be replaced at about 80,000 miles.

Pollution & Efficiency. We all know that EVs are supposed to be cleaner for the air, but some people wonder how accurate that is when the big picture is taken into account. Sure, there's no smoky tailpipe, but what about the utility generating plant?

It is much easier to clean up one utility smokestack than hundreds of thousands of tailpipes. Even including the pollution caused by generating the electricity, the EV is much cleaner than a gas car. *How much* depends on the source of fuel for the electric generating station. In California, where there is a great deal of clean hydro power, an EV is 85 - 97% cleaner than a gas car. Even in the east, where the power sources are less clean, an EV is 27% cleaner than a gas car.

It is important to realize that these numbers are based on new car emissions. Most of the cars on the roads, however, are older models that do not have as sophisticated emissions controls as the new cars. The contrast would be even more pronounced if EVs were measured against these typical older model cars.

The percentage of improvement goes even higher when you realize that gas cars are dirtiest on short trips when they don't get fully warmed up, and in stop-and-go driving——which is exactly the kind of driving they spend most of their time doing.

Finally, we must remember that every gas car, as it ages and deteriorates, becomes dirtier and dirtier. An EV, having no tailpipe emissions at all, stays as clean as it was the day it was 'born'. In fact, the utility power plants supplying electricity to the car are continually meeting stricter and stricter standards, so the EV actually gets *cleaner* the longer it stays on the road.

The next question is, "If we have a lot of electric cars, won't we have to build more power plants?" The answer is, "No." EVs charge primarily overnight, when utilities have excess capacity. By using that capacity, EVs help utilities level their demand load, and run their plants more cleanly and efficiently. A study by Southern California Edison indicated that the utility could absorb 600,000 EVs without increasing capacity. For scale, that means that if every Toyota sold in the whole country in 1987 had been an EV, and they had all moved to Los Angeles, they could have been charged from existing power plants. (This number also represents about 10% of the total cars in southern California.)

There are other automotive pollution issues that get less attention. For instance, every highway develops a dark streak down the center. This is not from tires (it's in the wrong place) but from the drops of oil and other fluids that leak out of cars. With every rain, some of this washes off the road, and is one of the major sources of groundwater pollution.

When a gas car is serviced, almost everything that comes out of it is hazardous waste: oil, coolant, oil filters, fuel filters, and so on. Many of the chemicals and solvents the mechanics must use are also classified as hazardous materials. Picture the pile of waste fluids and parts that comes out of a gas car in three to four years. In that same time, the only hazardous waste coming out of an EV will be from the battery pack when it is replaced. About 1% of those batteries——ten pounds—— will end up as hazardous waste that cannot be recycled or cleaned up.

There are other subtle sources of pollution, too. For instance, when a gas car is sent to the junkyard,

"Gas cars are dirtiest on short trips and in stop-and-go driving."

even after it has been stripped of re-useable and recycl-able parts, about 30% of the car ends up in the landfill as 'fluff': seats, interiors, etc. When a new car is manufactured to replace it, several tons of waste are generated in the manufacturing process. Doesn't it make more sense, instead of junking the car, to recycle the whole vehicle into an EV?

What about wasted energy? The energy used to manufacture that new car would be enough to power the average person's gas car for almost two years. They could use it to drive even longer in an EV. Although utility plants are not very efficient, they are much more efficient than gas engines. If you start with the mining of raw materials, and calculate through the processes of refining and transporting gas vs. generating and trans-mitting electricity, all the way to the wheels on the road, the EV is half again as efficient as the gas car. Only 11% of the energy in the crude oil in the ground makes it to the wheels of the gas car. By comparison, 17% of the energy in the raw materials (oil, coal, or whatever) makes it to the wheels of the EV.

Noise. Noise is also a kind of pollution. EVs are virtually silent. While older controllers had a high-pitched whine, the newer ones do not. The only sounds are the click of the main contactor, the faint singing of the motor, and the sound of the wind and pavement going past.

Night & Foul Weather Driving. Modern EVs are fully capable of night and rainy weather driving without an appreciable loss of range. Snowy, slippery roads that reduce traction will also reduce range. Cold weather will reduce performance as well. In cold climates, it is recommended to insulate the battery boxes, and possibly heat them during charging—-much as gas cars use block heaters. However, there are many happy EV owners in New England, Canada, and even Alaska, so cold weather need not be a hindrance.

So that's what an EV is and does. It's not a heavy work vehicle, or a vacation vehicle. It can be souped up as a race car, but that's not what this book is about. This book will help you build a reliable, economical, low-maintenance, clean car for daily use. It can be a sedate commuter, or a flashy show car, but it will be unusual and special. Now, if this sounds like what you want, let's get into specifics.

3

Safety

DON'T SKIP THIS SECTION.

I know, you're anxious to get started, and you already know all the basic safety rules. Take a minute to review them anyway.

Basic safety procedures should be practiced as a matter of habit. The one time you bypass them will be the time you get hurt. This is not meant to be a comprehensive list.

Eye Protection

Always wear eye protection when using power tools or handling batteries, or working near machinery. A full face shield is best, but safety glasses or goggles are the bare minimum. This is to protect your eyes from small sharp flying pieces, as well as from any accidentally splashed battery acid.

Power Tools

Know the proper handling techniques for the equipment you are using. Be aware of what is behind or underneath the area you're working on, so you don't saw through your power cord or drill into a battery. Use sharp saw blades, as dull ones will cause a saw to kick back. Check the rpm rating on grinding stones to be sure your drill doesn't exceed them. Be careful not to exert side force on drill bits.

Jacks & Stands

Get a good, heavy-duty floor jack, not one of the mini-jacks with the cute little wheels. Likewise, get solid stands that are made of at least 1/4" material, welded or cast, not those flimsy little stamped steel stands. They should be rated for at least 2 tons. This car will gain about 800 pounds before you're finished. If you're going to be under it, you want equipment that's up to the job.

Check your factory manual for the proper placement points. Keep in mind that these points might change with the conversion. You want to be sure you are actually supporting the car itself and not the battery box. Position the stands under frame members that won't deform when bearing the weight of the car. Lower the car gently to the stands. If the support point shows signs of crushing or moving, it is not a proper support point. If the car tries to tip forward or backward, the center of gravity has been shifted, and the stands will have to be shifted forward or backward to compensate. Have a flat, solid surface under your jack and stands. Set the handbrake, and keep the gearshift in neutral.

Engine Hoists

Borrow or rent a real engine hoist for the engine/

motor swap stage of the conversion. Do not try to cobble together a substitute using the kids' swing set or the garage rafters.

Check your factory manual for instructions. Make secure connections to the proper places on the engine, and be sure that your cable or chain has the proper strength for the job.

Batteries
Chemical Danger

Burns. Sulfuric acid, which is contained in the battery, will burn clothes, paint, tools, and most importantly, skin. Battery acid destroys cotton materials, so I recommend that you wear synthetic work clothes. Keep a box of baking soda handy. Use it to neutralize any spills immediately, then rinse with plenty of water. For further care of spills on skin or eyes, or ingestion of acid, call your nearest Poison Center or other emergency service.

Handling. To protect against accidental splashes, don't move batteries with the caps removed. Also, be aware that pressure on the endwalls of plastic-cased batteries can cause acid to spurt through the vents. For this reason, it is recommended to use a battery carrier to lift batteries. Be sure it grips the battery securely. The type of carrier with teeth that bite into the battery case works fine on old rubber case batteries, but not on the newer plastic cases. If you lift a battery by hand, grasp it at opposite corners.

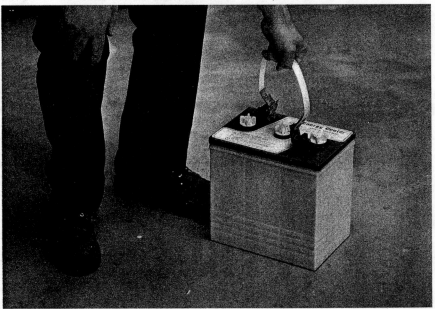

A proper battery carrier.

Explosion. Hydrogen and oxygen gases are released during normal battery operation, particularly at the end of the charge cycle. They are increased by rapid charging or discharging, or by overcharging. Hydrogen becomes explosive when it reaches a 4% concentration by volume. It is rare for a battery to explode, but if one does, it will scatter pieces of case and hot acid, and may start a fire. Most batteries now come with flame barrier caps. However, all sources of flame and sparks should be kept away from batteries, just as you would keep them away from your gas tank.

To avoid sparks, do not break a live circuit at the battery terminal. Instead, throw the circuit breaker and turn off the ignition key. Locate components that may produce sparks away from the batteries. Keep in mind that hydrogen is lighter than air, and will rise. For that reason, it is safer to locate some components below the level of the battery tops.

Leave the battery caps on during charging, and open the box lid or provide a fan for ventilation. If you use a fan, be sure it has an 'anti-arc' feature. This is a brushless fan, or one that is rated as safe for marine bilges.

If the batteries release a strong sharp odor, this is a warning. Turn off the charger and check it for proper functioning. If smoke, violent gassing, or spewing of electrolyte occurs, shut off the charger IMMEDIATELY and check the charger and batteries for defects.

Avoid leaning over batteries when possible. This protects you from injury, as well as reducing the chance that a tool may fall from your hand or pocket and short across the battery terminals. This would melt the tool, and could cause an explosion. If you must lean over the batteries, cover them with a fender cover, rubber floor mat, blanket, or piece of cardboard.

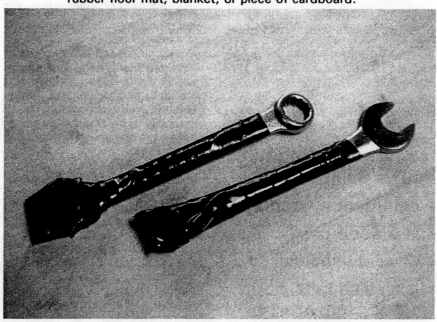

Insulated battery wrenches.

It's a good idea to have a pair of dedicated battery wrenches. One should have a box end exposed, and the other should have an open end exposed. The rest of the wrenches should be completely insulated, either with electrical tape or a plastic dip coating.

Containment. It is always recommended to enclose batteries in a box. If the batteries are inside the passenger compartment, this is absolutely required. It is also necessary to cage and secure the batteries to keep them from flying loose in a collision or rollover.

We'll talk more about containment in the chapter on battery racks and boxes.

Electrical Danger

Low Voltage System. This is the 12-volt system that powers lights and accessories. High current caused by a short can travel through your entire wiring system, damaging wires and components and possibly causing a fire. Always disconnect the auxiliary 12-volt battery at the negative cable when working on the 12-volt system. Use good quality wire and connectors of the proper gauge, and follow the techniques explained in the chapter on wiring.

High Voltage System. Isolate the high voltage system completely, so that it does not ground through the chassis at any point. This reduces the danger of shocks, as well as reducing the danger from failures of connections or insulation.

An interlock on your charger is a good idea. This will prevent the vehicle from being driven away while still connected to the power source.

I recommend three types of safety power disconnects, which operate manually or automatically. All three should be used together. The first is a main contactor. This is an electromechanical disconnect which is operated manually by your ignition key. This gives you a way to disconnect the batteries from the drive system when the car is parked, if you suspect a problem while driving, and during charging. It is part of the normal automotive operating procedure that we are all familiar with already.

The second safety disconnect is a circuit breaker between the battery pack and the main contactor, or within the battery pack circuit. This could be used manually as an emergency shut-off if the main contactor failed in a closed position. It will also operate automatically in an emergency such as a motor short, or in case of driver abuse if the car is being pushed beyond its abilities.

The circuit breaker must be rated appropriately for your battery pack and components. It must also be a DC circuit breaker, not an AC breaker. The operating characteristics of the two are different, and an AC breaker might not trip at the appropriate time in an emergency.

The third disconnect is a fusible link wired into the circuit between two of the batteries in the pack. If your battery pack is split between the front and rear of the car, as most are, I recommend a fusible link in each section. This is an automatic shut-off that will function in the event of a short circuit in the pack, which can be caused by a tool or piece of sheet metal making contact across the terminals.

There are actually two other emergency disconnects. One is a 'deadman' microswitch on the potbox which opens the main contactor whenever the throttle is completely released. The other is a good pair of cable shears. If all else fails, cut a cable.

"The final emergency disconnect is a good pair of cable shears. If all else fails, cut a cable."

Design & Technique

The subject of safety ranges from details like preventing the failure of a connection to broad-scope issues like handling, performance, and crashworthiness. Every step of the design of the conversion, and every technique used in building it, is integral to safety. We will be talking about safety-related design and technique issues throughout this book.

Safety Equipment

In any kind of vehicle, a safety kit is a good idea, even though you will probably never need to use it. In an EV, this should include:

1. A fire extinguisher. Be sure it is rated for electrical fires. CO_2 extinguishers leave no mess, but are bulkier and more expensive than dry chemical extinguishers. A sodium bicarbonate extinguisher is suitable for electrical fires, and will neutralize any acid spills as well.

2. A box of baking soda.

3. A pair of cable shears.

4. A crimper/stripper and a selection of connectors.

5. A bypass cable long enough to connect any two batteries in your pack, in case you have to remove a bad battery from the circuit.

6. A pair of insulated battery wrenches.

7. Extra fusible links. If you blow a fusible link on the road, you need to find and correct the problem that blew it. Then you need to replace the link in order to drive home.

8. Two each 1/2" and 7/16" combination wrenches for installing fusible links.

9. A volt/ohm meter. It should have a scale of at least 0 - 150 volts. Very nice digital ones about the size of a deck of cards are available for $20 - $30.

10. A flashlight.

11. Flares.

Remember, safety rules only protect you if you use them, and there is no substitute for common sense.

"Every step of the design of the conversion, and every technique used in building it, is integral to safety."

4

"You do not have
the resources
to build components
comparable to
to those available
commercially,
and the potential
safety risks
cannot be justified
by the money
'saved'."

What You Need To Get Started

Space

Ideally, you would have a two-car garage or the equivalent that you could dedicate to the project for the duration. In real life, if you have one stall you can take over completely, you're doing well. Many of you will have to share a garage space with a gas car, or other activities. This will entail a certain amount of regular exercise as you push the donor car in and out.

Set aside an area to store the internal combustion components until the conversion is done. Don't dispose of anything, except possibly the engine itself. There is a wealth of brackets and raw materials in that pile that can be re-used in the conversion and save you hours of fabrication.

It's helpful if you also have a single staging area where you can lay out all the conversion parts you will be using. You will be handling these parts many times during the design phase, before they are actually installed.

You will also need a work area sufficient for fabricating pieces as large as battery boxes.

Time

The amount of time you spend on the conversion will depend on the completeness of the kit you use. On the low end, a completely pre-fabricated bolt-in kit can be installed by an experienced mechanic in as little as 32 hours. For the average automotive hobbyist, this might stretch to four weekends.

For a kit in which you are responsible for component layout, and design and fabrication of battery racks, boxes, and miscellaneous component mounts, you should plan on at least 200 hours. Most of that time will be spent on design of the overall layout and specific mounts.

Components

The following is a typical list of components for a conversion. Trying to cut corners by eliminating any of these is not recommended, as it will compromise performance and/or safety. I also do not recommend building any of the components other than battery boxes and racks and miscellaneous mounts and brackets. You do not have the resources to build components comparable to those available commercially, and the potential safety risks cannot be justified by the money 'saved'.

> Motor
> Adaptor
> Controller & Potbox
> Charger
> Main Contactor
> Circuit Breaker
> Fusible Links
> Ammeter & Shunt

Voltmeter
DC/DC Converter[1]
Power Brake System[2]
Shocks & Springs[3]
Clutch Parts[4]
Battery Racks[3]
Battery Box(es)[3]
Cable
Lugs
Batteries[4]
Miscellaneous Component Mounts[3]
Miscellaneous Wiring [3]

[1] Optional, but highly recommended.
[2] Only necessary if donor car had power brakes.
[3] Will be included in bolt-in kits only. For other
    kits, you will have to source these parts yourself.
[4] Generally not included in kits.

Before we move on, I'd like to say a word about buying kits vs. separate parts. There are several advantage to buying a kit, besides convenience. First, you know that all the components are compatible with each other. When buying components separately, especially older models of components, it is possible to get combinations that will not work together.

Second, it is usually cheaper to buy a package than to buy the same pieces separately.

Third, there are sometimes tax incentives attached to kits that are not available for separate components.

It may be possible to get a good deal on used parts through an electric car club. However, the buyer must use extreme caution to be sure the parts will provide satisfactory performance, are compatible with each other, and represent a real cash savings after all the other necessary parts have been collected. I do not recommend used parts for a beginning electric vehicle enthusiast.

Suppliers

The electric vehicle industry is experiencing another surge of interest. This means many people who have little background in EVs are suddenly buying cars and components, and many other people with equally little background are suddenly selling them.

I have a unique perspective on the EV industry, since I have been in it since 1979. I watched the spurt of interest rise—and fall—with the last gas crisis. I stayed in the business through the slow years of 'cheap' gas when everyone else folded their tents and moved on. I believed the time for EVs would come again, and stay. Now I am watching many of the same mistakes being made again that were made last time.

Those of us in the industry have a duty to educate the buying public about possible pitfalls. Whenever someone has a bad experience with an EV or an EV business, it tarnishes us all. Whether you buy your components from me at Electro Automotive or elsewhere, there are certain principles that will help insure you get a 'good deal', meaning quality and value for your dollar.

With that in mind, I would like to offer the follow-

"When you buy your components, there are certain principles that will help insure that you get quality and value for your dollar."

ing guidelines for those trying to sort through the various claims and offers of electric vehicles and components.

Get References. Never take the word of a salesperson on its own merit. Check with independent knowledgeable sources in the industry, such as electric vehicle enthusiasts' clubs or alternative energy publications. Is this person or business well-known and established within the industry? How long have they been involved with EVs? Are they reliable, ethical, and competent?

Any industry in a boom phase will attract a swarm of new 'businesses'. Some will be outright frauds, though they may be extremely smooth and convinvcing. Others are honest and sincere people who simply don't have the technical or business background to deliver on their promises. Dealing with an established, reputable business will insure technical support for the components you buy.

These are some phenomena that should be approached with caution:

The Instant Expert. Just because an EV is relatively simple, many people think no special expertise is needed to be an expert. This person may claim to have been in the EV business for ten years. On independent research, however, you will find that no one in the industry heard of him before last year. He's been 'in business' for ten years—installing car radios—and he's had an EV or two that he bought used and tinkered with from time to time. This person knows just enough to cause serious problems.

Rip Van Winkle. He really has been in the EV industry since ten years ago. In fact, he's *still* in the EV industry of ten years ago. His components are three generations behind the times, and will not give satisfactory performance. Surprisingly cheap prices are often a warning sign of this situation.

The Hobbyist. Some hobbyists are brilliant, and should be declared national treasures; others should be declared national disasters. Be sure to find out from outside references which kind you are dealing with. Also be aware that you may end up with a one-of-a-kind vehicle that is only fully understood by its creator, and is a mystery to everyone else. Such an orphan can be a problem if you ever need to make changes or troubleshoot a malfunction.

Magical New Components. Someone has always 'just come out with' a Magic Motor, a Better Battery, or some other Holy Grail that will give amazing range and power, weighs almost nothing, produces more power than it uses, and cures cancer. On closer inspection, you will find that these fantasy components are hand-built laboratory prototypes. They also have a few little drawbacks, like enormous price tags, 600° F operating temperatures, or a tendency to self-destruct. Someday some of these fairy tales will come true, and will benefit us all. In the meantime, it is foolish to base your vehicle on the magic of tomorrow. If you do, your dream coach-and-four will remain a lumpy pumpkin pulled by white mice. Build with available technology today. You can always upgrade later.

"Some hobbyists should be declared national treasures; others should be declared national disasters. Be sure to find out which kind you are dealing with."

> **"Components that are too cheap or too expensive will prove to be unsatisfactory."**

In general, be realistic. An EV built with proven, current production technology can provide completely satisfactory performance for use as a local commute and errand-running car. This represents the largest percentage of American daily mileage, and is the perfect niche for the EV today. Components that are too cheap or too expensive will prove to be unsatisfactory. Take a little time to learn who is established, respected, and experienced in the industry, and you will be treated well.

Cost

The minimum cost for a sound conversion using new modern components is about $5,500 - $6,000. In this instance, you will not be using a bolt-in kit. You will be doing the component layout design, and designing and fabricating all the necessary battery racks, boxes, and miscellaneous mounts. This price assumes using the least expensive materials that are adequate for the job, such as plywood for the boxes.

The high end cost for a basic conversion is about $8,000 - $9,000. This is for a pre-fabricated bolt-in kit including better quality materials such as powder-painted battery racks and welded polypropylene battery boxes.

Your costs may fall somewhere between these two if you use a non-bolt-in kit, but better quality materials.

You can easily spend $50,000 on a conversion if you want to use high-tech drive systems or exotic batteries, but this is completely unnecessary.

I should say a word here about tax incentives. I won't get too specific, because these change from state to state and from year to year. Simply be aware that there may be some tax breaks to help you finance your conversion. Contact the nearest electric car club to find out what is currently available in your area.

For example, California passed a law effective in 1991 that established tax incentives for conversions. (The law was cleverly given zero publicity, but we found out about it anyway.) Basically, the law stated that a conversion kit (if duly certified by the state) was exempt from sales tax, and eligible for up to $1,000 in state income tax credits. The law will lapse in 1995.

When we called the state to find out how to get our kits certified, they couldn't answer us. No one had bothered to figure out how to implement the bill. My partners and I, especially Dick Rahders, spent many hours wheedling and badgering the state into writing the procedures to implement the law. We were the first company to get our conversion kits certified. Now, it's a simple matter of filing a couple of forms and visiting a smog referee to collect a tax credit.

Other states may have similar or other incentives, including sales tax exemptions, income tax credits, registration incentives, and even insurance subsidies. There are also some federal incentives in place, and others on the drawing board, but it is not clear whether these apply to conversions by private individuals or only fleet conversions and new vehicle purchases.

Check the current incentives in your area. If there aren't any, call your state legislators and ask why not.

Page 23

Advisors

There are a few people in your town who can be valuable advisors on this project. They include the dealership parts man, a good aftermarket parts man, a wrecking yard man, and a welder. They may also include a machinist or plastic fabricator.

(And by the way, some of the best parts 'men' I have known have been women.)

In dealing with these people, be as professional as possible. They are often harried and overworked, and they deal with more than their share of vague and confused customers. Always go in armed with complete information. This means, besides make and model, any special designations ('DX' or 'GT'), body type (2-door, 4-door, hatchback, wagon), and the Vehicle Identification Number as extra insurance.

The engine size will be important, even though you are throwing the engine away, because many other parts such as brakes and suspension are keyed to the engine size. The exact production date (month and year) can be important, especially on Japanese cars, since there may have been running production changes. This date can usually be found on a metal plate somewhere on the driver's door or door pillar. The parts men may ask seemingly irrelevant questions, such as, "How many headlights does it have, and what shape are they?" Believe it or not, this may help you get the right clutch parts.

The best plan is to explain your project briefly, show them this manual, and get them personally interested in and excited about your conversion. A bag of cookies or a box of doughnuts can also help cement your relationship.

The dealership can help you get specific details on your car, and identify possible useful crossovers from other models. Some parts are available only from dealers.

For other parts, an independent aftermarket parts house can offer the same kind of help. Look for a store that caters to the trade, with a lot of guys in blue uniforms as customers. There will be at least one person in that store with a wealth of product knowledge in his head. Franchise stores that sell to the public usually have staff who only know what's in their catalogs and computers.

A wrecking yard can be a cheap source of the interchange parts that you identified with the help of your friends at the dealership and parts house.

Welders, machinists, and plastic fabricators can build mounts and boxes for you, but they can also assist in the design stage by recommending types of materials, construction techniques, and explaining the strength requirements to do the job properly.

Books

There are two books that are essential for your conversion. The first is the factory—repeat, *factory*—manual for your make, model, and year of car. This is the same manual the dealership issues to its mechanics. An aftermarket manual will not be specific enough, especially for things like wiring diagrams. The factory

"The factory— repeat, *factory*— manual for your make, model and year of car is essential for your conversion."

"Your Project Notebook will be the 'factory manual' for your conversion."

manual will guide you through the disassembly of the internal combustion system, provide a road map to the existing 12-volt system, and assist you in other mechanical work, such as brakes and suspension.

The second is a Project Notebook. Use something you're comfortable with: a spiral notebook, three-ring binder, blank bound book, or whatever you like. Reserve it for this project alone, and keep it where you can always find it easily. You will need to make notes and drawings and jot down measurements as you work on the car. Keeping them all in one place will make it easy to refer to them later. Be sure to label your drawings and make your notes detailed enough that they will still make sense to you in a couple of weeks—or a couple of years. What you are building is the 'factory' manual for your conversion.

A third book is highly recommended. This is *Battery Book One,* written and published by Curtis Instruments, Inc. This book will give you a detailed picture of how lead-acid traction batteries work, and how to optimize their performance. This book is available through Electro Automotive.

Tools

The following is a recommended list of tools and supplies. If you are an automotive hobbyist, you will have most of them already. Some of the specialty tools may be included in your kit, or may be available from your kit supplier. Many of the tools will not be needed if you are installing a bolt-in kit.

Large Tools
    Engine hoist & sling (can be rented)
    Floor jack (min. 1 1/2 ton rating)
    Heavy duty stands
    Sawhorses
    Creeper

Power Tools
    Electric drills (3/8" drive & 1/2" drive, with drill
        index 1/16" to 1/2" by 1/64" increments, hole
        saw attachments, and unibit)
    Jigsaw (Milwaukee Sawzall-type tool preferred if
        available, with 32-tooth metal-cutting blades)
    Circular saw (with plywood blades and cutting
        guide)
    Hand grinder (with metal grinding wheel and sanding
        disks)
    Heat gun or hand-held propane torch

Hand Tools
    Razor box knife
    Cable crimper
    Cable shears
    Wire stripper & crimper
    Small soldering iron
    Hammer
    Pliers
    Combination end wrench set (8mm - 19mm metric or
        3/8" - 3/4" inch, to suit your car)
    3/8" drive ratchet and sockets (same metric or inch
        sizes as end wrenches)
    Allen sockets (3/8" drive, 5/32" & 5/16" sockets)

Tap & die set
Assorted sizes flat & crosspoint screwdrivers
Diagonal blade wire cutters
Pry bar
Hacksaw
Coping saw
Steel measuring tape (at least 18')
Steel straightedge (48")
Metal square
Scribe or ice pick
Center punch
Punch set
Chisel set
Pop rivet tool
Torque wrench
Caulking gun
Dial caliper
Battery lifting strap
Battery wrenches (two 1/2" combination end wrenches, all but one end on each wrapped with electrical tape)

Miscellaneous Tools
Safety glasses or goggles
Drop light
Volt/ohm meter
Bench vise
Drain pan
C-clamps
Broad felt-tip marker
Leather gloves
Yellow tire crayon
Shop towels

Supplies
Assorted cable ties
Anti-corrosion compound (such as Noalox or Cual-Aid)
Shrink tube
Spray carburetor cleaner
Silicone spray
Red Loctite
Moly lube
Caulk
Heatsink grease
Masking tape
Duct tape
Spray primer and paint
Mechanic's wire
Low friction synthetic transmission oil
Teflon thread-seal tape or paste
Drywall screws
Construction panel glue
Blue layout fluid

Now the stage is set. It's time to choose the donor car.

5

Choosing A Chassis

One does not convert a car, like climbing a mountain, just because it's there. Some vehicles make better conversions than others. Let's start talking from the broadest scope, and work our way down to specifics.

First, I want to limit the discussion to passenger cars, pickup trucks, and light vans. Large and small industrial vehicles can be converted to electrics, as can ultralight racers, motorcycles, and bicycles. However, all these vehicles fall outside the range of this book, and need to be addressed separately elsewhere.

Ground-Up Design

In an ideal world, an electric car would be designed and built from the ground up to maximize efficiency and performance. In real life, however, this is not a practical option. The average person, even a very talented and experienced one, does not have the expertise or resources to design and build a complete vehicle. A ground-up design requires not only the frame and body, but brakes, suspension, steering, doors, headlights, and a multitude of tiny details—all of which must meet certain standards to be street legal. If you are an automotive or industrial design professional, you may be able to do it, but it will consume enormous amounts of time and money.

Simply converting an existing car provides plenty of opportunities for you to exercise design and fabrication skills. Take advantage of the chassis and mechanical design that some manufacturer has already done, and concentrate your efforts on the conversion aspects.

The Vortex is a car you build from a set of plans. It's built from the ground up, but the design work has already been done for you. (Photo courtesy of Dolphin Vehicles.)

Kit Cars

If you are a very hands-on person and want a more ambitious project——and a more unusual final product——you can build a kit car as an electric. Their lightweight fiberglass bodies make kit cars excellent performers as electrics. Since you assemble the entire car from pieces, you have the opportunity to make minor modifications to the chassis to aid in the conversion.

The Jackrabbit kit car is a high quality kit, and can make an excellent electric. (Photo courtesy of Herb Adams VSE.)

If you are interested in building a kit car, do some serious research before buying your kit. Be sure you are buying from an established and reputable supplier. Ask for references from customers who have the kit you want. Try to see a finished car in the flesh, so you can check out the quality of the kit, and its potential as an electric. Find a local kit car club and get advice from more experienced builders.

Most of us will be converting existing gas or diesel steel-bodied cars. There are several aspects of the car to be evaluated before making a choice.

Weight

Increased weight decreases range and performance. The same heavy cars that get poor gas mileage will make poor electrics. Look for a car that's under 2,500 pounds curb weight before conversion. Under 2,000 pounds would be even better, and 3,000 pounds is the upper limit. Remember that, even after stripping out the internal combustion components, the car will gain 800 pounds or more during the conversion.

The curb weight is what the car actually weighs when it is empty. Gross vehicle weight is the maximum rated weight, fully loaded. To check curb weight on a potential donor car, go to the library and look up *Road & Track Magazine* for the year the car was built. There will probably be a detailed report with all the relevant specs. *Consumer Reports* also carries such information.

While lightweight cars are good, they may have their

own problems. One is limited space for batteries. Even a very light car needs a minimum of 72 volts, which means twelve 6-volt batteries, to be marginally street safe, and 96 volts, or sixteen batteries, is recommended. Another potential problem is the ability of the suspension and frame to accept the added battery weight.

The ideal chassis is light but roomy, something similar to a Rabbit, Civic, Sentra, Escort, or light pickup truck. Beware of cars like the Fiero, that are actually much heavier than they look.

Light pickup trucks, like this Datsun, make good conversions.

Body Style

Look for accessible battery space. Hatchbacks are probably the best choice. Remember that batteries can be sunk into the floor. This means you can have batteries and a backseat, too—and even cargo space in the hatchback area, on top of the battery box.

Check the engine compartment for protrusions or a low-profile nose that might interfere with battery placement.

Age

The rule of thumb here is to look for a car that is less than ten years old, and the newer the better. There are many reasons for this. Newer cars obviously offer better crash protection and aerodynamics, since much progress has been made in these areas in the past decade. Also, availability of parts is poorer after ten years, and drops significantly after fifteen years for many cars. Even after the car is converted, you will still need things like brake pads.

Condition

The ideal donor car has a good body and interior, sound transmission, but a dead engine. For these reasons, cars like the diesel Rabbit make an excellent choice. Watch the classified ads for ones that say, "Good body, needs engine." Also, talk to local junkyards or independent garages that specialize in the kind of car you want, and tell them to watch for a good candidate for you. Specialty mechanics may be able to recommend a particular model of car that tends to blow up engines.

If at all possible, get a mechanic to check out the donor before you buy it. You will want to know about the brakes, transmission, and constant velocity joints, as these are the most likely items that can add expense to the project. The clutch, shocks, and springs aren't as important, as you will be changing those anyway. Be on the lookout for any evidence of crash damage that might have tweaked the frame. A small variation from 'true' in the chassis can sometimes drive you to distraction when you are trying to mount components to it.

If you get a donor that runs, you can recoup some of your investment by selling the engine. This is best done while it's still in the car and can be test driven. Be sure the buyer knows that you will be keeping some of the parts, such as the flywheel.

Make & Model

The first criterion for make and model is availability of parts. Look for a make with a strong dealer presence in your area, and a model with a long production run and a large number of them built and sold. This will mean availability of dealer-only parts and expertise, of aftermarket parts, and of junkyard parts. Orphans make poor candidates for conversion, even if Aunt Minnie has one behind the barn that she'll give you for free. However, a twenty-year-old car might still be a good candidate if it's in good condition and there is good parts availability.

This Rabbit is more than ten years old, but there is still good parts availability for it because there were so many of them built.

In general terms, it is harder to find a suitable American donor than it is to find a foreign one. This is because American manufacturers have only recently become interested in producing small aerodynamic cars. They are often American in name more than content. Japanese cars seem especially suitable for conversion.

A few cars have special idiosyncrasies. If you get a Honda, be aware that the crankshaft rotates in the opposite direction from almost every other car in the world. Your electric motor supplier should be able to adjust the motor so that it runs most efficiently in the proper direction for your car.

Subarus and rotary Mazdas have a design that recesses the flywheel into the back of the engine. This requires a very thick and expensive adaptor plate for the electric motor. For that reason, I don't recommend them.

Transmission & Drive Axle

Conversions can be front-wheel drive or rear-wheel drive. Having the engine and the driving wheels at the same end of the car makes packaging easier, but isn't essential. Four-wheel drive is not a practical option at this time.

Automatic transmissions are also not practical for individual conversions at this time. They can be done, but performance is marginal and they can't really be economically justified except for fleets. One problem with automatics is a loss of power, which electrics can ill afford.

Another problem is that an automatic transmission depends on a continuously idling motor to provide fluid pressure. Without it, there is a serious lag in acceleration from a full stop. An electric motor doesn't idle. When the car isn't moving, neither is the motor. If you idle the electric motor like a gas engine, you are wasting energy and defeating its efficiency. Adding a separate fluid pump adds one more component and level of complexity to the system.

Finally, electric motors have a different torque profile and want different shift points from those of a combustion engine.

I wouldn't be surprised if there is a suitable automatic transmission for an electric car in the next few years, but it isn't here yet.

We do maintain the original clutch and flywheel in the conversion. One reason is safety. If anything should go wrong while the car is in motion——a motor lockup or runaway, a locked-up wheel——it is possible to disconnect the motor from the wheels using the clutch. Another reason is comfort. Using the clutch gives a much smoother ride.

Another drive option often suggested is direct drive, or even a motor on each wheel. I do not recommend either option. Direct drive can be done, but it is expensive and bulky. Without a transmission, an enormous amount of voltage or current is needed to achieve a combination of good acceleration and highway speeds. Most direct-drive cars use packs of more than 300 volts, which means a lot of batteries. It also means very expensive components, and special charging requirements.

Motors on the wheels themselves have design problems

"Using the clutch gives a much smoother ride."

due to the unsprung weight of the motor. Multiple motors need very tricky synchronization of speed controls and steering.

Options

In general, a 'Sally Rand' (stripper) version of a car is preferable to the luxury version. Air conditioning eats almost as much horsepower as it takes to move the car down the road. Also, air conditioning technology is now in a state of transition, due to the CFC problems. Probably within the next few years a new air conditioning system will emerge that is environmentally benign, and suitable for an electric car.

Power steering is another energy eater, but most of the potential donor cars in a suitable weight range don't have it anyway.

Luxury models also usually have more sound deadening, which is not necessary in an electric car.

Power brakes, on the other hand, are easily accommodated with a vacuum pump, and are highly recommended, due to the added weight of the batteries.

Power windows and stereos don't use enough energy to hurt anything. Enjoy.

The Right Stuff

There are three ingredients in a good electric conversion: a good chassis, the right components, and a well-designed and carefully executed installation. Just because a particular car is readily available or cheap does not mean it's suitable—and a poor chassis will give you a poor EV. Making the right choice at the beginning will go a long way toward a satisfactory final product.

"A poor chassis will give you a poor EV."

6

Removing The Internal Combustion System

Before you can install the electric components you will have to remove a lot of original equipment. Which pieces you remove—or save—and how you do it can make a big difference in the final conversion.

When Detroit builds a car that is 70% new design and 30% off-the-shelf, it spends 3.1 million hours of engineering design time on the 70% of the car that's new. For optimum results in your home-built electric car, it makes sense to take advantage of as much of that engineering as possible.

Measurements

There is one basic rule that is essential when disassembling something that must be reassembled later: study, measure, and mark everything BEFORE you take it apart.

Therefore, when you are ready to start disassembling, the first things to save are measurements. With the car parked on the level, measure the ride height at all four wheels and record these numbers in your Project Notebook. This is done by running a steel measuring tape vertically from the ground, across the center of the wheel, to the center of the wheel arch on the body.

Measure the ride height at all four wheels before you start stripping the car.

There will be some difference in these measurements, front to rear and side to side. Knowing what these differences were before conversion will let you know whether any differences after conversion were there originally, or introduced in the conversion process. Incidentally, if the initial difference is greater than 2" from side to side, check for possible frame damage from an accident.

Page 33

If the car can be driven, get it weighed——the whole car, and each axle separately. This will help you try to match the original weight distribution and adjust your suspension.

The first piece to remove is the hood. Before you do, use a scribe to trace the outline of the hinge in the paint on the underside. This will make it easier to reinstall the hood precisely later. A slight misalignment can cost you hours of tinkering while you try to get the hood latch to work properly.

Before removing the engine, measure the distance from the top of the transmission bell housing to some mark on the firewall. If your car has a transverse-mounted engine, lay a flat piece of steel or wood across the fenders at a point you can mark and duplicate later, and measure straight down from this piece to the bell housing.

Measure the distance from the top of the transmission bell housing to some stationary mark. (It's easier to see in this photo, with the electric motor already in place, than in the original car with the gas engine.)

This measurement will help you reinstall the transmission with the electric motor in exactly the same position. This is important for such things as driveshaft angularity and shift linkages.

Another thing to study before disassembly is the throttle linkage. Make notes about how the pieces go together, and measure the travel distance from full off to full on at both the pedal and the carburetor or fuel injection system. These measurements will be critical when installing your electric throttle connections.

IC Component Removal

Now you are ready to start removing the internal combustion (IC) components. Use your factory manual to guide you through this process, incorporating the additional following instructions.

The first things to throw away are all the fluids in the old car, except hydraulic fluids. Brown's First Law of Conversions states that any car you choose for a donor will have a fuel tank that's more than half full. If the fuel is clean and fresh, it can be used in some other IC vehicle.

Drain the engine oil and the radiator fluid. (Note: on the west coast, this is called 'coolant'. In the midwest and east, it is called 'antifreeze'. Same fluid. Climate determines semantics.) The transmission oil should be drained, too. When you reinstall the transmission, you will want to fill it with a low-friction synthetic oil.

Dispose of all the fluids carefully and properly. This is especially important with coolant. It is sweet and attracts small children and animals—and it is a deadly poison.

If any of the factory manual instructions seem strange, complicated, or require you to remove or disconnect unrelated things, check with a shop that specializes in your make of car, and see what procedure they use. There may be a be a better way, or a special trick. For example, the Rabbit factory manual says to remove the engine from the bottom of the car, but we always took it out from the top when I worked in the dealerships.

When the engine and transmission have been removed from the car and separated, there is one more measurement to take. I call this the 'magic number'. This is the distance from the rearmost surface of the engine (where it mates to the transmission) to the rearmost flat surface on the flywheel. This may or may not be the friction surface of the flywheel. The measurement should be accurate to three decimal places in inches.

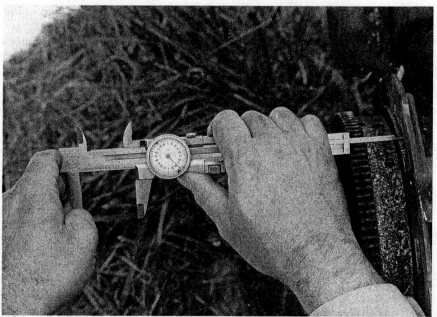

The 'magic number' is the distance between the rearmost surface of the engine and the rearmost flat surface of the flywheel.

If there is already a pattern on file for an adaptor for your transmission, this number is unnecessary. However, if I have to design an adaptor, I will need this number to determine the thickness of the hub.

As you take the donor car apart, do so with a scalpel instead of a machete, because you might want to graft some of those pieces back together later. Remove all the wires at their connectors instead of cutting them, and label them with tape and a marker. Be sure it

Page 35

is an indelible marker. Otherwise, you may steam clean the engine bay and end up with lots of pretty little white flags with no writing on them.

As you disconnect wires, label them with tape and an indelible marker.

Save all the original nuts and bolts in baggies, and label what they came from. These may allow you to re-use original holes or brackets.

It is generally easier to remove both the engine and transmission, then reinstall the transmission later with the electric motor mounted to it. You may think it's less work to leave the transmission in the car, but it actually makes your job harder.

There are two metal tabs on the engine that are specifically for lifting it with an engine hoist. Save those tabs and adapt them to your electric motor, adaptor, and transmission when it is time to sling them into place.

Even if you are replacing the clutch, save the old parts until you are sure the new ones match. Save the flywheel and all the bolts associated with it, because you will want to re-use them with your adaptor. These are special bolts, and will cost you time and money if you have to special-order them through the dealer. Also save any locating dowels between the engine and transmission.

Remove everything associated with the IC system: radiator, fuel system, exhaust, etc. You will want to use a 12-volt accessory battery, but not the original one. If you do not have a DC/DC converter, you will want to replace the original battery with a heavy-duty deep cycle battery, especially if you do much night driving. The DC/DC converter is highly recommended as a constant source of voltage for lights, etc., but it doesn't re-place the battery. If the DC/DC should fail for some reason, it will do it at night ten miles from home. So if you do have a DC/DC, you will still want a 12-volt battery, but you can use a very small one.

Don't plan to eliminate the 12-volt battery by tapping across two of your main pack batteries for accessories. This will cause uneven discharge of the pack, and shorten its lifespan. It also violates the rule about isolating the traction batteries from the auxiliary battery and chassis.

When the car is apart, this is the time to inspect things like constant velocity joints and boots, and replace them if necessary. This is also the time to steam clean the engine bay in preparation for installing the nice clean electric components.

As you disassemble your donor car, take notes on anything you may need to reassemble later. Use your Project Notebook for sketches and diagrams. Maybe you'll want to take photos or videos. Use whatever method works best for you, but document everything.

The building of the electric conversion actually begins with the dismantling of the internal combustion car. If it's done right, the process of disassembly is an integral part of the process of assembly. It should be done thoughtfully, with the vision of the finished conversion always in mind.

7

Installing The Motor & Adaptor

The motor is the center of the electric car's universe. It is the first component you need to install. It has a pre-determined position in the center of the engine compartment, and all other components must fit in around it. The type of motor you use will determine what other components you use, and what performance you will get. It is not the place to skimp.

Motor Types

In the rugged early days of the modern electric car (meaning the late 1970's), the aircraft generator or starter was the most common motor used simply because there were few other options readily available. It made a great aircraft generator, but a very marginal electric car motor. It was rated at 24 volts, but for automotive use it was run at 48 to 72 volts. Not surprisingly, the generator often refused to take such abuse and died. Also, the rpm band of the generator was not suitable for a car, causing it to suck up great rivers of amperage, which translated to a short driving range.

These generators are still emerging from basements with 'For Sale' signs, but they are less appropriate than ever. For one thing, the shaft has a 16-tooth spline that's very expensive to mate to an adaptor. For another thing, they are incompatible with modern controllers.

Another motor of yesteryear was the Baldor. These had a disturbing habit of spontaneously disassembling themselves.

An interim motor of the mid-1980's was the China Motor. Designed as an improved version of a aircraft generator, it operated well at 72 volts, but not higher, and it had the same spline problem.

The series brush DC motor is the favorite for conversions.

The motor of choice for the hobbyist today is the series DC motor. The most popular line is manufactured by Advanced D.C. Motors, Inc. It is efficient, reliable, readily available from various distributors, affordable, and most important, it is designed to be an electric car motor. This motor dominated the 1992 Solar & Electric 500 race in Phoenix.

Other usable motors are the Prestolite and G.E. The Prestolite is the forerunner of the Advanced D.C. motor. It is a little larger, heavier, less efficient, and less well ventilated, but if cost is a factor and a used Prestolite is available, it will serve you well. This motor is no longer in production.

The G.E. motor (*not* the same as a G.E. aircraft generator!) is also adequate, and has approximately the same slight drawbacks as the Prestolite. If you are buying a used G.E. motor, be sure to check the rpm rating. It should be 5100. There are still some in circulation that are only rated at 2300 rpm. They have lots of torque, but no top end speed.

What about other types of motors: shunt, compound, permanent magnet, brushless DC, or AC? All of these suffer from limited or non-existent availability in sizes suitable for cars. Shunt and compound motors have less acceleration than series motors, and permanent magnet motors have a narrower rpm band of efficiency. This means that they are most efficient at a constant speed. This makes them perfect for something like an ultralight cross-country solar racer, which maintains a steady pace. In normal driving, however, speed varies greatly. Permanent magnet motors are least efficient at the low rpm used most in stop-and-go driving.

Brushless DC and AC motors are available primarily from a company called Solectria in Massachusetts. While they are slightly more efficient than series motors, their control systems are much more expensive. They are good equipment, but are generally used only in production and race cars, and very high-end hobbyist cars.

Then there are the various exotics. These are at the opposite end of the spectrum from aircraft generators. Most of these are the unproven dreams of tomorrow. They are laboratory animals, available only as hand-built test prototypes. They are still being debugged, and are not commercially available in regular production. Eventually, some of them will certainly mature into valuable EV components, and you can always upgrade to them. Until then, don't design your electric car around something that is still a pipedream.

If you are converting a Honda, be sure to inform your supplier when you buy your motor. Honda engines rotate in the opposite direction from everything else. Some motors can run in either direction. On the Advanced D.C. motor, the supplier can make an adjustment so that the motor will be most efficient in the right direction. Some motors will not work in this reverse application.

Adaptors

Once you have your motor, you need to install it in the car. The first step is attaching it to the transmission with an adaptor.

"A chain is only as strong as its weakest link, and so it is with an electric car's drivetrain."

A chain is only as strong as its weakest link, and so it is with an electric car's drivetrain. All of the horsepower and torque needed to move the car down the road must pass through the adaptor on its way to the transmission and wheels. This, like the motor, is no place for half measures.

The adaptor needs to be designed, machined, and installed precisely. This does not mean laying the transmission face-down on a piece of cardboard and tracing the outline and holes with a pencil to make a pattern. A professional adaptor manufacturer will measure and machine each bolt or dowel hole, as well as the thickness of the plate itself, to be accurate within a few thousands of an inch. This kind of accuracy assures a secure fit between motor, adaptor, and transmission. Any sloppiness in fit will eventually cause poor performance and could damage the motor or transmission.

Okay, let's look at what an adaptor is. There are two sections to an adaptor: the plate that mounts the motor to the periphery of the transmission, and the hub that connects the motor shaft to the flywheel and physically transmits the power. The plate can be made of aluminum in order to save weight. It should be no less than 5/8" thick for adequate rigidity.

The plate may actually come in two parts, as long as they are precision machined to fit together. At Electro Automotive, we use a 5/8" thick transmission profile plate and a motor ring that varies from 5/8" to 2 3/4" in thickness.

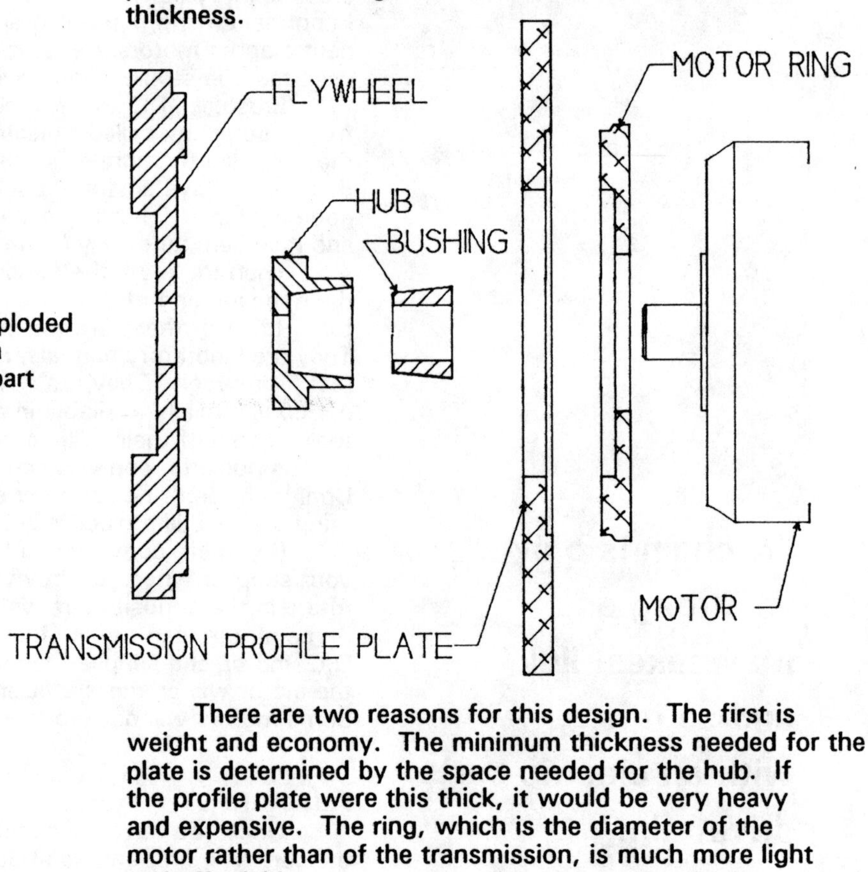

This diagram shows an exploded view of an adaptor using a two-part plate and a two-part taperlock hub.

There are two reasons for this design. The first is weight and economy. The minimum thickness needed for the plate is determined by the space needed for the hub. If the profile plate were this thick, it would be very heavy and expensive. The ring, which is the diameter of the motor rather than of the transmission, is much more light and affordable.

The second reason is that it allows the car to be upgraded to a newer or larger motor by simply changing the ring, instead of the entire adaptor.

The other section of the adaptor is the hub. This connects the motor shaft to the flywheel. This must be made of steel, not aluminum. The motor shaft has a square steel key in it that fits into a slot in the hub. If the hub is soft aluminum, that steel key will eventually 'egg out' the slot and start cutting into the hub like a machine tool bit. This is not a pretty sight, especially at 50 mph.

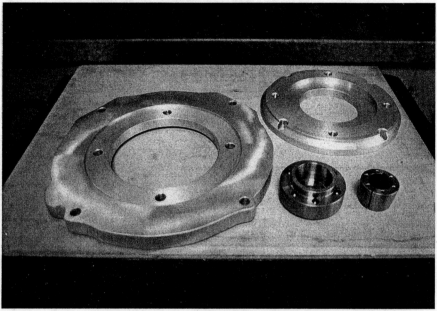

An adaptor, showing the transmission profile plate, the motor ring, the motor shaft bushing, and the hub.

There are several styles of adaptor hubs. Most of them are problems waiting for the worst possible time to happen. All the power of that motor passes through this little hub the size of a hockey puck. This, also, is not a place to skimp.

One style holds itself in place with a setscrew through the side of the hub. Another uses a flat washer and a bolt in the end of the crankshaft. These both have the same problem: threads loosen. It doesn't matter how much Loctite you use. It will eventually work loose, and you'll be a pedestrian.

A third style is the shrink fit. In this type, the hub is heated very hot, then slipped over the shaft and allowed to cool and shrink into place. This will give a good, secure connection. Unfortunately, it's too secure. If you ever need to remove that hub, you've got a problem.

The last style is a taperlock. This, like the plate, comes in two pieces. One is a cone-shaped bushing that slides over the motor shaft. It also slides inside the second piece, a hub that mounts to the original flywheel. The cone has a slit through it, and starts out a little bigger than the hole it fits into, so it won't go in all the way. As screws are tightened to pull it in, it compresses the slit and squeezes the motor shaft. It's easy to install, but once it's in place, the only way it will come off is with a special pulling tool.

Page 41

This taperlock style of hub is the most secure for an electric vehicle, and is the standard for high-torque high-rpm industrial power shaft connections.

There are some numbers that need special attention here. The first is the 'magic number'. On the gas or diesel car, this is the distance between the back of the motor and the rearmost flat surface of the flywheel. This distance needs to be duplicated when installing the flywheel on the electric motor.

Measuring the 'magic number' when installing the adaptor

The second number is a measurement of torque. The hub is attached to the flywheel using the original bolts. These are special hardened bolts. When installing them, use a torque wrench and the torque numbers in the manufacturer's service manual.

A motor secured to the workbench with a chain, eyebolts, and turnbuckle.

In order to get the leverage you will need to tighten these bolts, the electric motor needs to be immobilized. One way to do that is by using one or two very muscular friends. A better way is to strap the motor to the workbench. This can be done by installing sturdy eyebolts in the workbench on either side of the motor. Then pad the top of the motor with shop towels, and run a length of chain between the eyebolts and across the motor. Tighten the chain with a turnbuckle until the motor doesn't move. Also, use a steel anti-rotation strap attached to mounting holes in the commutator end of the motor.

An anti-rotation strap installed on a motor for bench work.

Any time you are tightening a circular pattern of bolts, make several passes over the entire sequence, and use a criss-cross pattern. That is, don't try to tighten one bolt all the way, then the one next to it, and so on. This will cause the piece you are installing to tilt slightly, and you will not get a proper tight fit when you are finished. You may even damage threads.

When tightening bolts in a circle, use a criss-cross pattern, tightening each bolt a little bit, and making several passes over the whole pattern.

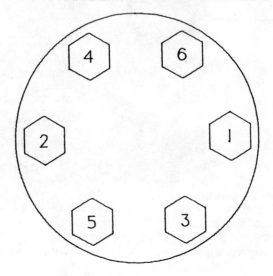

Instead, tighten one bolt by just a couple of turns, then move to a bolt across the circle from it, then across again to a new bolt. Tighten each one only a little bit each time, and make several complete passes until all bolts are adequately tight. Use a consistent pattern to be sure you aren't missing any of the bolts.

Flywheel & Clutch

We discussed earlier why we still use a transmission and clutch. Now let's talk a little about the flywheel.

The flywheel has a safety function. If you were to over-rev the motor with no load (flooring the throttle with the car out of gear, for example), the motor could 'run away' and self-destruct. The flywheel provides just enough load to help protect against that.

Some people suggest lightening the flywheel to improve drivetrain efficiency. There is some advantage to this. The most benefit would come from removing the ring gear, which is no longer needed. The spinning flywheel teeth actually create some drag through air turbulence. This modification is not really necessary for the average conversion, though. It's something for electric vehicle hot-rodders to play with, since they don't have carburetors anymore.

There are some reasons not to alter the flywheel. Too much lightening will dangerously weaken the flywheel. Also, it may be impossible to find a local machine shop capable of doing this specialized work.

If there is a hot-rodders' machine shop in your area, there is one trick I would recommend. Have the flywheel and clutch balanced together. This will give you smoother performance.

Clutch parts being mounted on the motor and adaptor. (Note flywheel lock tool at top, and paint mark for aligning flywheel and pressure plate.)

The flywheel is part of the clutch assembly. When you are installing the adaptor, this is the time to replace the clutch pressure plate, disc, and release bearing with new parts. If you do it right the first time, you won't have to change the clutch again until you replace the motor brushes at 80,000 miles.

Motor Mounts

Now it's time to install the entire motor/adaptor/ transmission assembly in the car. When you disassembled the car, you took some measurements to lock in the original position of the transmission. You want to duplicate that position when you install the electric motor. This is essential for proper shift linkage and driveshaft angularity, among other things. Any change in the position of the transmission will impair smooth efficient performance.

Motor/adaptor/transmission assembly ready to be installed in the car.

In order to do this, you will need to design your motor mount precisely. In most air-cooled Volkswagens, no motor mount is necessary. The electric motor hangs off the transmission, just like the original gas engine did. For all other cars, read on.

Use a floor jack to raise the assembly until the transmission is back in its original position, as verified by the measurement you took from the top of the bell housing. Now design your motor mount to fill that space between the motor and the chassis.

You can make a mock-up of a motor mount from cardboard or foamcore. Make your mock-up with the same precision you would use for the real thing. When you think you have something that will work, take your mock-up to a welder for fabrication. (Better yet, see if you can get him to visit your garage and look at the mock-up in place.) Solicit his advice on any reinforcing straps or gussets.

As with any other metal mounts, the finished piece should get several coats of a good corrosion-resistant paint as a minimum.

There are two types of common motor mounts. One is a cradle that supports the motor around the middle, with a strap over the top. This is appropriate for a car with an in-line engine. This type of mount arrangement also

Page 45

requires a torque rod to brace the motor against spinning in its cradle.

Try to use the original chassis motor mount brackets. If their placement would cause the cradle to interfere with terminals on the motor, it is possible to build small offset plates to go between the chassis brackets and the cradle, in order to shift the cradle forward or back to a better position. It may be necessary to install a support member either above or below the motor to serve as anchor for the cradle.

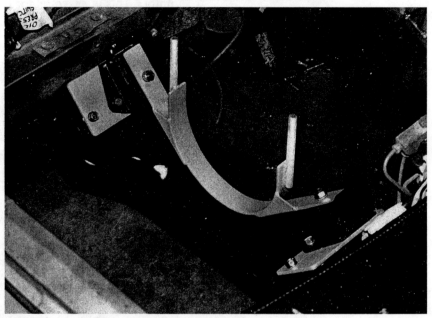

A cradle-type mount, mounted to original (black) motor mounts, and (grey) setback plates.

For a transverse engine car, use a plate mounted to the anti-drive end of the motor and extending into a mounting bracket.

A mount for a transverse motor.

There may be some bolt heads exposed on the case of the motor. DO NOT loosen these or in any way try to use them for your mount. They hold the field coils in place inside the motor, and they are installed at a specified torque. Loosening them will cause damage to the motor.

The original motor mounts are 'metalastic' pieces. That is, they have a rubber part bonded to a metal frame. This is great for reducing vibration and noise, so you should use the same technology. Design your mount to attach to these mounts. If the original mounts aren't too misshapen, use them for your design phase, then buy new ones for the actual installation. If the original style of mount won't work, try to find another style from a different model of car at your auto parts store.

Keep the motor commutator covered with a cloth or masking tape while you are working on the car, to prevent any tiny chips or debris from falling into it and damaging it. During driving, normal road splash will not be a problem, but you shouldn't try to ford any puddles that might actually immerse the motor. A small amount of belly shielding is recommended, expecially in areas where roads are salted or gravelly.

Be sure the shielding does not obstruct airflow for cooling. If it does, duct air from another area to the motor. Prestolite and G.E. motors should have an external cooling fan. This is not necessary on the Advanced D.C. motor.

Torque Rods

We mentioned a torque rod earlier. A cradle-type mount circles the motor but does not actually bolt to it. Under power, the motor will try to rotate in place. A torque rod is needed to counter this force.

The easiest way to build a torque rod is to adapt one that someone else already produces. A Honda torque rod is good. This is a dogbone-shaped piece: a straight rod with two rounded ends with bushings in them. The larger end can be unscrewed.

A Honda torque rod modified for use in an EV

Install the torque rod between the chassis and the

Page 47

nearest bolt hole on the motor-side top edge of the adaptor. Locate the torque rod so that it will not interfere with anything else. Build a U-shaped bracket to allow you to bolt the small end of the torque rod to the chassis.

Unscrew and remove the large end of the torque rod and replace it with a bolt with a nut on it. Build an L-shaped bracket to connect that bolt to the bolt on the motor adaptor. The bracket should go between the bolt head and the nut. You can adjust the length of the torque rod by adjusting the bolt in the threaded end of it. Lock it by tightening the nut against the bracket.

Once the motor is installed, it's time to move on to batteries.

8

Batteries & Containment

One of the biggest components in an electric car is the battery pack, in many senses of the word 'big'. It is the bulkiest and heaviest component. It is one of the most expensive. And it is one of the most important to performance.

Which Kind Of Battery?

Designing the battery pack involves a series of decisions. The first decision is which kind of battery to use. If you study the literature about EV batteries, you may feel overwhelmed by myriad possibilities. In reality, though, the choices are not that broad.

The 'miracle' batteries that receive so much attention——sodium sulphur, lithium polymer, nickel iron, etc.——are simply not commercially available to individuals. They may be planned for production for manufacturers only, or available only as laboratory test prototypes, or they may be nothing more than computer projections——vaporware. The same thing is true of fuel cells, such as hydrogen or zinc air.

Therefore, the first question to ask about any type of battery is, "Where can I buy one?" The answer for most of the exotics will be, "Nowhere——they aren't available yet."

The second question to ask is, "How much will it cost?" Some batteries are available——like nickel cadmium, or silver zinc——but only at costs equaling or exceeding the entire rest of your conversion expenses. If you are planning to build a dedicated race car, batteries with a high price or limited lifespan may be worth it for superior performance on the track, but they don't make sense for a daily driver.

Unless you have special contacts or a lot of money, the answers to these first two questions will probably narrow the field to conventional lead-acid batteries.

Performance Characteristics

The third, and most complicated, question to ask is, "Are the performance characteristics of the battery well-matched to the needs of an EV?" This question has several different aspects. The shape, number, and spacing of plates, composition and thickness of lead paste, and the ratio of electrolyte to paste are all critical items that vary depending on the intended use of the battery.

For example, the normal battery used in a gas car is a starting battery. It is intended to supply high current for a very short time——just long enough to start the engine. It is discharged by a small percentage, then immediately recharged by the alternator. It is never intended to be deeply discharged, and especially not repeatedly. As many of us have found out, a starting battery that is run 'dead' too often, perhaps by leaving the lights on accidentally, will soon refuse to revive.

An EV needs a deep cycle battery. This means it can be discharged to 80% of its capacity and recharged

"An EV needs a deep cycle battery."

Page 49

repeatedly. Conventional starting batteries and other non-deep cycle batteries such as gel cells can provide high short-term performance for a race car, but not continuous daily use.

Traction Batteries

Not all deep cycle batteries are appropriate. Marine batteries or standby power batteries are not intended to handle the occasional brief current peaks a car requires. They will not provide as much range or cycle life as a true 'traction' battery.

A traction battery is designed for high current draws *and* repeated deep discharges, both of which are needed to move a vehicle down the road. The type of battery most commonly used in EVs is a golf car battery: a 6-volt deep cycle battery, typically rated at 220 - 240 amp/hours. This is an excellent choice because it is well-developed, very available, and affordable.

Lead-acid batteries: the new 12-volt traction battery, and the conventional 6-volt golf car battery.

There is also now a true traction 12-volt battery available from U.S. Battery. This is the model 1450, which can be ordered through U.S. Battery or Interstate dealers. While this battery is too new to have full life-cycle testimonials from EV owners, it was developed by a company with an excellent record of producing quality batteries suited to EVs. The 1450 would be highly recommended for very small cars where space is limited, and may well eventually take over the market for larger conversions as well.

Ni-Cads

Nickel cadmium batteries are probably the second most common in EVs, far behind lead-acid. There are several drawbacks to ni-cads. One is high cost, even for reconditioned batteries. Another is low energy density. It is necessary to have several strings of ni-cads in parallel to have sufficient amperage capacity for accel-

Page 50

eration. This means a lot of space filled by batteries.
A third problem is that ni-cads come in 1.2-volt cells,
which require many more interconnects—and potential
failure points—than golf car batteries.

For most people, the conventional 6-volt lead-acid
deep cycle golf car battery is the optimum choice today.
If a better battery becomes available next year, you can
always upgrade to it.

Post Styles

There are three common battery post styles. The
first is the automotive style we all recognize from our
gas cars. This is a large round stud, which is gripped
around the outside by the cable end. These provide good
surface contact area, but the cable ends are bulky and
expensive.

The second type, called the universal style, is most
common because it is popular in golf cars. This is just
like the the automotive style, with the addition of a
threaded steel stud sticking up out of the center of the
post. It is connected by placing a lug on the end of the
cable, and fitting the lug over the steel stud and holding it in place with a nut.

This is the worst possible style. Its failings are
not as critical on a low voltage golf car, but can be
disastrous in a full passenger car. First, the top of
the post offers a small contact surface area. Second,
the post is subject to 'cold creep'. This is the process
by which lead will flow at room temperature while under
pressure. The pressure of the nut will cause the steel
stud to loosen and creep upward inside the lead post. If
the loose connection is not found, it will cause resistance. Resistance generates heat, which can melt the
lead post and start a fire.

If you are careful to tighten the connection often,
then the steel stud will simply work its way up until it
comes all the way out of the post.

The preferred style is the 'L' terminal. This is an
L-shaped post with a flat vertical tang, which has a hole
in it. It provides good contact surface area for lugs.
When we get to the wiring section, we'll discuss techniques for making snug connections that won't loosen
under cold creep.

How Many?

Once you know what kind of battery to use, the next
decision is how many. In simple terms, amps equal torque
and volts equal speed. However, you can't simply add as
many batteries as you want. Each one is the size of a
toaster and weighs close to 70 pounds.

Early EVs often ran 48-volt systems. The industry
is still trying to live down the poor performance they
had. A 72-volt system is the bare minimum for a road-
going passenger car. This will give performance comparable to that of the original gas-powered 1200 CC VW Bugs.
It will only be adequate for a very lightweight car that
is never intended to be driven at highways speeds.

As we noted earlier, most conversions have a 96-volt
system, which means sixteen 6-volt batteries. This seems

Automotive style battery post.

Universal style battery post.

'L' style battery post.

to be the optimum weight/power balance. A typical steel-bodied conversion will have a range of 60 - 80 miles in average commute conditions: mostly flat roads, some freeway time, some stop-and-go in-town traffic. It will have a top speed of about 60 mph. Some of the more aero-dynamic cars will do better. A lighter weight fiberglass car will have a range of 80 - 100 miles on a charge and a top speed of about 90 mph.

If there is room for the batteries, the system can go as high as 120 volts. In fact, this is recommended for pickup trucks, where some payload capacity is desirable. Very soon there will be chargers and controllers available for systems up to 144 volts. However, the advantages of the extra voltage will have to be weighed—literally—against the expense, bulk, and weight of the extra batteries.

When To Buy Batteries

Although you have chosen the batteries you will use and decided how many you want, don't buy them until you are ready to install them. Get precise dimensions and use cardboard or foamcore mock-ups for designing your car. That way the batteries won't be going stale sitting on your garage floor for weeks or months—and you won't be tripping over them.

Single Or Split Packs

One of the first design decisions in converting a car to electricity has to be where to put the batteries. In a typical car, there are sixteen to twenty of them. All other design decisions will depend on where the batteries are placed, and how they are oriented. The obvious consideration is available space, but other important factors include weight distribution and current path.

The Voltsrabbit™ has a typical split pack, with eight batteries under the hood in a split-level arrangement, and eight behind the back seat.

For stability and handling, the ideal arrangement would be to have all the batteries in a single block, between the axles. This can be done in a van by sinking them into the floor or building a false floor above them. In a pickup truck, the batteries can ride in the bed, but a better plan is to tilt the bed and install the batteries underneath it. This gives good handling and also maintains cargo space. Some of the batteries may be placed under the hood as well.

In a passenger car, the batteries almost always end up split between the front and rear of the car. Weight should be kept inboard of the axles as much as possible, and balanced between the front and rear. If either end is significantly heavier, handling will be poor. The weight should also be kept as close to the ground as possible for a stable center of gravity.

In the engine compartment, it makes more sense to keep the batteries grouped together as much as possible in the large open center area and distribute the components around the periphery, than the other way around. This arrangement makes it much easier to design the racks, boxes, and wiring.

It is perfectly acceptable to cut into a chassis to sink the batteries, if it is done with proper care. No structural members should be cut or weakened. Any time you cut into sheet metal, it should be primered and painted to protect it against rust.

The batteries should be enclosed in a sturdy welded rack. This will reinforce any area where the chassis was cut. Care needs to be taken to insure that the batteries do not interfere with axles, suspension, etc., and that they do not extend downward far enough to diminish road clearance. Once the batteries are installed, use caulk or duct tape to seal openings between the rack, box, and chassis to restore weatherproofing and reduce road and wind noise.

A rear battery rack recessed into the floor behind the back seat.

Accessibility is also a consideration in battery placement. You will want to be able to get to the batteries fairly easily to inspect the terminals and connections and check the water levels. For this reason, you don't want to stack batteries on top of each other.

Current Path Layout

Once you have a general idea of how you would like to place the batteries, you need to lay out the circuit path and get the positive and negative terminals oriented correctly. On the next page is a sample battery layout diagram from the Voltsrabbit™.

Following that are two pages of 'tools' for you to use. These are scale drawings of the U.S. Battery model 2300 6-volt and model 1450 12-volt batteries. Photocopy the page that matches the batteries you are using, and cut them out. Coat the back of each battery with Dennison 'Tack A Note' adhesive. This will allow you to stick them into a battery box drawn on a piece of paper according to the layout you have planned. Then you can take them off, rotate them, and stick them back on until you get the right orientation.

The 'most positive' cable out of the pack will connect the main contactor to the positive terminal of the battery you declare to be first in the string. The batteries are then connected in series, positive to negative, like a daisy chain. If the pack is split in two or more locations, the last negative terminal of one location will be connected by cable to the first positive terminal of the next location. Finally, the 'most negative' cable will come from the last negative terminal in the entire series and go to the speed controller.

Check your intended layout. Are any of the interconnects long or awkward? Do any of them interfere with each other, or with the battery caps? (Note: find out in advance what style caps your batteries will have.) Do the most negative and most positive cables come out of the circuit anywhere near the contactor and controller?

Try to keep interconnects and cable runs as short as possible, although sometimes long runs can't be helped. Avoid complicated or criss-crossing interconnects. With these thoughts in mind, re-examine your layout, and see if turning some of the batteries 180° will simplify the circuit. If not, maybe turning some of them 90° into a slightly different configuration will help.

Component Locations

Obviously, you will be deciding the locations of some of your components in the course of designing your battery layout. As mentioned earlier, you need to know where your controller and main contactor will be in order to plan the battery connections to them. It is more important for them to be close to each other and to the motor, than to be close to the cables from the battery pack.

Circuit breaker placement is also a factor. Ideally, the circuit breaker interrupts the most positive cable between the batteries and the main contactor. If this is not practical, it can be placed between any two batteries in the series. It's best to locate the circuit breaker within easy reach of the driver. If it is

"Try to keep interconnects and cable runs as short as possible."

Voltsrabbit™ Battery Layout Diagram

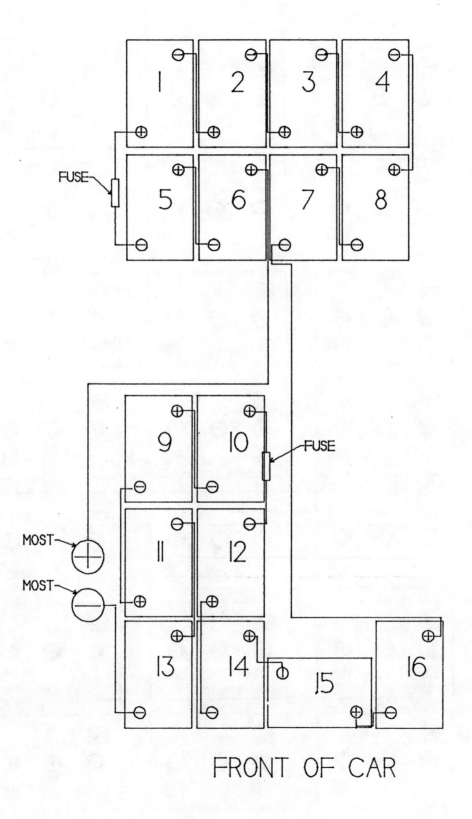

FRONT OF CAR

6-Volt Battery Layout Dummies
U.S. Battery Model #2300

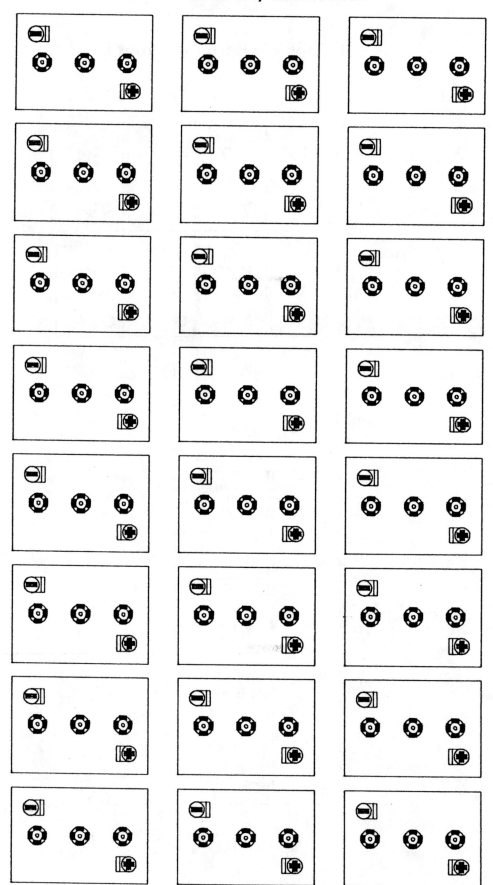

12-Volt Battery Layout Dummies
U.S. Battery Model #1450

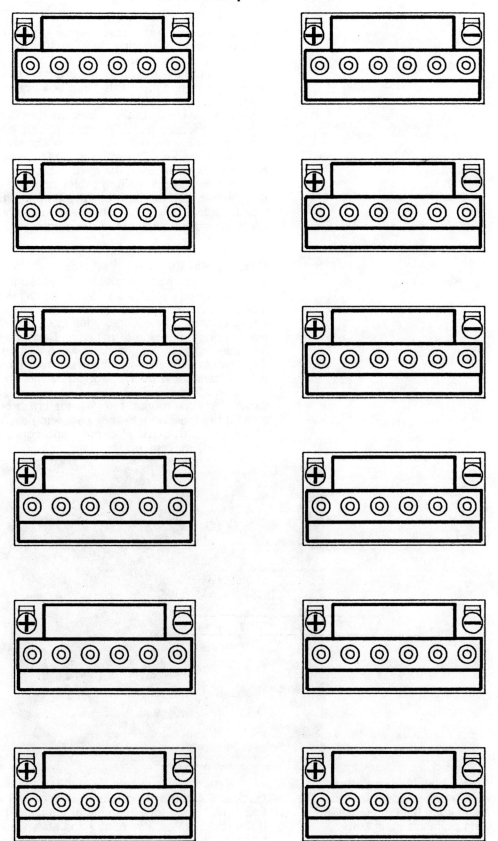

Bold lines indicate raised areas of the plastic battery case that might interfere with interconnects.

located away from the driver, some kind of reliable remote method of flipping the switch is needed.

In our Voltsrabbit™, it worked out that eight batteries fitted under the hood in a strange, split-level arrangement, and eight fitted in a box behind the back seat. The most positive cable ran from the main contactor under the hood, to the circuit breaker in the dash, to the rear battery box. The most negative cable from the rear box connected to a positive battery terminal in the front batteries. The most negative cable of the overall pack emerged in the front, near the controller.

When you are running cables fore and aft like this, it is advisable to run both positive and negative cables side by side. This will diminish electrical noise that could interfere with some of the components.

Battery Racks

Once you have juggled all these factors into a satisfactory layout, you are ready to start designing the racks and boxes to secure these batteries in place. All batteries should be secured adequately to stay in place, even during a collision or rollover. Don't be fooled into thinking their weight alone will hold them in place. Department of Transportation crash test tapes of early electric cars show poorly secured batteries sailing into the air in 30 mph barrier tests. Watching batteries fly forward in slow motion to crush the crash test dummy against the steering wheel is a sobering experience. Other cars with better placement and containment suffered little battery movement.

Voltsrabbit™ front battery rack and holddown frames. The frames are held in place with long stainless steel bolts.

Battery racks should be made of welded steel angle stock and straps with minimum dimensions of 3/16" thick and 1 1/2" wide (or a material of equivalent strength). If the rack is large, use reinforcing straps across the bottom. If you are not trained as a welder, hire someone else to do the work. Your battery racks are not the place for on-the-job training.

Additionally, the batteries or boxes need holddowns across the tops. For boxes, these can be bars or rigid straps bolted into place. For batteries not enclosed in boxes, it is necessary to have an angle-stock frame that encloses their tops and is bolted down. A simple strap across the top without an enclosing box will not be adequate to keep batteries in place against the sharp lateral force of a collision. Of course, the holddowns must be placed so they cannot accidentally short across two terminals. The following are NOT suitable holddowns: plexiglass, nylon straps or belts, plastic shipping straps, and ready-bolt.

As a minimum, racks must be painted to prevent rust and corrosion. You can do this with spray paint, but the best option (if you can afford it) is powder paint. This paint is applied as an electrically charged spray powder to an oppositely charged part. The powder will actually flow around corners to coat evenly and fill small spaces. It is then baked to a tough, ceramic-like finish which is both non-conductive and corrosion resistant.

A nice added touch is a thin sheet of plastic on the bottom of the rack (if there is no box) covered by a layer of Battery Mat. This is a felt-like material impregnated with acid neutralizers. Placing it under your batteries will help protect the rack from accumulated battery acid mist. If your rack is not powder-painted, this material will also provide some electrical insulation between the batteries and the rack.

Battery Boxes

Batteries should be enclosed in boxes whenever possible. It is absolutely essential if batteries are inside the passenger compartment. The box will improve performance by regulating battery temperature. In an

This plywood box design has a multi-layer bottom, with a notch along the edges for the side boards.

accident, it will protect both the batteries and the passengers. In operation and charging, it will keep fumes away from the passenger compartment.

Page 59

For economy, the box can be made of plywood and then painted. Plywood is readily available and easy to work. The recommended thickness is 5/8", and 1/2" is the absolute minimum. Plywood can be assembled using construction cement followed by sheetrock screws. A good technique to use with sheetrock screws involves two drills. Use the first to drill pilot holes, and the second to install the screws with a screwdriver bit.

From your battery box design, make a list of each plywood piece needed, its thickness, and dimensions. Now make a scale drawing of a full 4' x 8' sheet of plywood, and mark off the pieces you need, in scale. Remember that you will lose about 1/8" with each cut of the plywood due to the width of the cut itself. Do your layout starting with the biggest pieces first, and work down to the smallest pieces, in order to reduce waste. From this drawing, you can determine how much of each thickness of plywood you will need.

Mark each piece on the plywood just before you cut it, according to your drawing, using a felt pen, a square, and a straightedge. Always measure from a factory edge of the board, not a cut edge. If possible, cut your pieces with a table saw, using a plywood blade. If you don't have access to a table saw, use a circular saw with a plywood blade and a plywood cutting guide.

Label each piece immediately on the rough side, which will be the inside. Use a ballpoint pen or pencil here, as a felt tip may bleed through your paint later. Labels should be detailed, like 'rear box, bottom side, this edge front'. In a layered construction, you may also need to include 'bottom layer'.

As you assemble the box, apply construction panel glue to each contact surface and have an assistant hold the board in place. Check for true corners with a square and then screw the boards together.

Plan to take the finished boxes to a packing and moving company and have them banded with steel packing straps at two levels for reinforcement. There are plastic corner protectors that can be placed between the bands and the box to prevent the straps from cutting into the wood.

As with battery rack paint, there is a better but pricier option: welded polypropylene. This material is stronger than plywood, so you can use as little as 1/4" thickness with proper rack support under and around it. It doesn't need to be painted, and is acid-proof. (In fact, it is used industrially for acid bath tanks.) It is lightweight, and makes an attractive package. You can get these boxes made at a plastic fabrication shop.

Batteries should be held down inside the boxes as well. If you hit a bump at speed, they can fly up against the box lid. To prevent this, attach small blocks to the lid at the corners of the batteries. When the lid is closed and strapped down, the blocks will hold the batteries down inside the box.

The box itself can be bolted to the rack beneath it using large carriage head bolts, which are recessed into the bottom of the box so they don't interefere with the batteries. This is not recommended for 1/4" thick plastic boxes, and should not be considered a substitute for holddown straps across the top of the box.

"Batteries should be held down inside the box as well."

A polypropylene battery box.
Note holddown straps.

Insulation, Heating, & Ventilation

In colder climates, it is recommended to insulate or heat battery boxes. Insulation can be done with 1/2" sheets of polyurethane foam inside the box. Do not use styrofoam, as it reacts badly with battery acid. If space permits, insulation can be built into the battery box floor and lid as well. There are battery heating blankets (available for use in large diesel trucks) that can be adapted to a battery box and plugged in like a block heater. Be careful that any heating system does not harm plastic components, or the Battery Mat.

A two-layer battery box bottom, with insulation.

Insulation can be simply a second layer between the box and batteries, or it can be a third layer in the middle of a 'sandwich' box wall or floor. In the two-layer version, it will be necessary to have supporting strips of plastic or wood secured to the box bottom around the edges and at intervals across the middle. These strips will support the actual weight of the batteries, and the insulation will fit in the spaces between strips.

The three-layer sandwich will only be possible in larger conversions where there is plenty of room. This will require a plywood bottom layer, an insulating layer with supports as described above, and a plywood top layer.

Batteries enclosed in boxes need to be ventilated, especially in the passenger compartment. There is a slight danger of explosion from collected hydrogen, although this is very unlikely. More importantly, we want to remove gasses that encourage corrosion and are unpleasant to passengers.

During driving this can be a passive ventilation system, since little gas is produced. Openings placed to catch the normal airflow can flush out most gases. Since hydrogen is lighter than air and rises, ventilation holes need to be along the top edges of the box. During charging, however, active ventilation is required. Use a non-arcing fan, such as one that is approved for marine bilge use. The most convenient and safest arrangement is to wire the fan so that it comes on automatically whenever the charger is engaged.

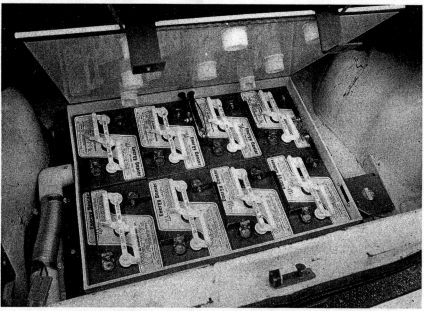

Rear Voltsrabbit™ battery box, with ventilating fan at lower right and exhaust duct at left. Note holddown blocks welded to inside of lid.

PVC fittings can be very useful for ventilation ducting. Elbows of various diameters and degrees of bend are available, as well as adaptors to fit round hoses to square holes. Aluminum Volkswagen accordion hose and clothes drier hose are both useful options.

While you're cutting holes in the battery box for ventilation, remember to also cut access holes for your cables.

Checking Dimensions

Once you've chosen your battery layout and rack and box options, it's time to start on a specific design. In your plans, add 1/16" to each dimension of each battery. The reason for this is that batteries swell as they age. If they are fitted too snugly at the beginning, it will be impossible to remove them when they are worn out. I know of one pack in which the center battery had to be emptied of acid with a siphon, then cut up and removed in pieces.

Before you start actually fabricating racks and boxes, check your dimensions against reality. Add the thickness of the battery rack and holddown material, the thickness of the box material and any insulation, the dimensions of the batteries themselves, and the 1/16" per battery allotment for swelling. The total of all these measurements should give you the maximum dimensions of your pack.

Now build a dummy pack to those dimensions out of cardboard or foamcore. Install it in the car and see if it fits, with the hood in place and closed. You may find surprise interferences such as hood reinforcements. If so, it's better to find out now, and make the necessary adjustments.

Temporary Installation

Once your battery racks and boxes are designed and built, install them loosely, but don't install the batteries yet. The racks and boxes will be useful for placing other components and wiring, but there will be times when it is easier to work on the car if they are taken out.

9

Installing EV Components

When designing your component layout, start with the bulkiest components or those which require special locations, then fit smaller and less critical components around them.

When possible, try to take advantage of original factory mounting holes and hardware. If you must drill a hole, be careful of what you are drilling into, and what is behind it. Use bolts and nylock nuts instead of sheet metal screws, to prevent vibration loosening. If you cannot drill a through-hole for a nut and bolt, you can use rivnuts or pop rivets.

A rivnut is a small metal tube that is installed in a hole like a pop rivet. It is threaded inside, and once installed, can be used like a captive nut to receive a bolt.

As always, I will concentrate on the components that are most commonly used in conversions today. If you have bought an older EV, or are using less common components, some of the finer details given here may not apply.

Motor Cooling Fan

This will only be necessary if you are using an older motor, such as a Prestolite or G.E. The bulk, noise, power consumption, and cost of a cooling fan are all good reasons to use a newer motor (such as the Advanced D.C.) which doesn't need one.

If you do need one, the best option is to mount it directly to the motor air intake. If you need to drill holes to do this, block all openings so that no chips can get into the motor.

If there is not sufficient room to mount the fan to the motor, mount it elsewhere nearby and duct the air to the motor. Be sure the fan and ducting are high enough to be protected from road hazards.

Speed Control System

The controller is to the electric car what the carburetor is to the gas car. It meters out the 'fuel' to the motor according to the demand, as signalled by the throttle pedal.

Controllers have advanced more than any other part of the electric car over the years. The most primitive system involved series-parallel switching. In this method, the batteries could be run in two configurations: all in series for full pack voltage, or split into two equal half-packs connected in parallel. This system had two speeds, which combined with the manual transmission to yield a confusing set of choices. It had complex wiring and required flipping some type of switch as well as shifting gears. It provided little speed control, and performance was jerky.

A second type of controller used resistors. This type could provide several speeds. At low speeds, the unneeded energy from the batteries was burned off as heat by banks of resistors. As each bank of resistors was

"Controllers have advanced more than any other part of the electric car over the years."

eliminated from the loop, more energy made it to the motor and speed increased. As you can guess, this system was extremely inefficient because the batteries were essentially always at full-throttle, but most of the energy was being siphoned off and wasted. It created a terrible fire hazard as well.

The SCR controller was an enormous improvement. It controlled speed by rapidly turning the battery voltage on and off, using a silicon-controlled rectifier. This type of controller is called a 'chopper'. The power is actually full on or full off at any given moment, but the pulses happen very rapidly, so the effect is an averaging out of the power.

The SCR controller simplified the wiring and gave a smoother and more complete range of speeds. However, it still lost efficiency through heat, and required a bypass contactor to achieve full throttle.

The SCR controller was both frequency and pulse width modulated. At higher speeds, it functioned by varying the duration of the 'on' part of the cycle—the pulse width—while holding the frequency constant. At lower speeds, however, it also needed to vary the number of times—the frequency—that it turned on and off each second. This ranged from about .02 kHz (kilohertz, or 'thousand cycles per second'), to about .4 kHz. This frequency range is audible as a growling sound.

Unfortunately, the SCR controller had some efficiency losses, and they tended to be worst right in the middle of the performance range, where most real-life driving is done.

The next step in the evolution of the controller was the transistorized pulse width modulated (PWM) chopper. When this type of controller was introduced by Frank Willey, and then further developed by Steve Post at PMC, it quickly dominated the EV market.

The transistorized PWM controller varied speed by varying only the pulse width, operating at a constant 2 kHz frequency. This was a much higher frequency than

PMC controller evolution: the early model DCC 96, the long-popular model 21, and the current MOSFET model 1221.

that of the SCR, and reduced noise to a slight whistle.

The transistorized PWM controller was smaller, lighter, quieter, smoother, more efficient, more reliable, and simpler to install than the SCR controller. Later models came in sealed weatherproof aluminum cases with extruded heatsink fins.

Since then, the PWM controller has evolved again. The Darlington transistors inside it have been replaced with MOSFETs (metal oxide semiconductor field effect transistors). The result is a more streamlined package without the heatsink fins, a broader range of input voltages, and a higher frequency of operation (15 kHz), which makes it virtually silent.

The company has evolved also. PMC is now a division of Curtis Instruments. They manufacture more than 200,000 MOSFET PWM controllers a years, for applications ranging from wheelchairs to large industrial vehicles.

A PWM controller is the best choice (preferably the MOSFET version), but an SCR controller is acceptable. In fact, SCR controllers are still used in very large motor applications, such as diesel/electric trains and electric transit trains. If you have an SCR, you will need to accommodate its larger bulk. Since its contactors and components are all exposed, you should provide some kind of weatherproof enclosure, while still allowing cooling airflow.

Resistor and series-parallel systems are not acceptable.

The controller should be mounted with its terminals as close to the motor terminals as space permits. On the PWM controller, the terminals can face in any direction except straight up. In that position, it is possible for moisture to collect and seep along the terminals into the controller and short it out.

I like to mount the controller, main contactor, and shunt all on one component board, which is then mounted in the car. These three components want to be mounted close together, and the detachable board allows me to do

A controller, contactor, and shunt, mounted on an aluminum component board which also serves as a heatsink for the controller.

the interconnecting wiring on the workbench in comfort, then mount the entire assembly into the car.

For the early (transistorized) PWMs, this component board can be made of wood or plastic, and mounted on the side of a battery box by installing tee nuts into the box. Tee nuts are threaded inserts that fit into holes drilled into the plywood, similar to rivnuts on metal surfaces. They act as nuts, allowing you to use bolts on a wooden structure. Be careful that your hardware does not interfere with the batteries inside the box.

For this type of mount, I also installed two studs on the outside of the battery box. Their only purpose was to fit into two holes in the component board and support its weight, leaving both my hands free to install the mounting bolts.

The MOSFET PWM controller disperses heat through its base, and must be mounted on an aluminum plate measuring at least 12" x 12" x 1/4". The plate need not be square, so long as there is that quantity of aluminum in it. A larger plate can be used, which can double as the component mount board. Coat the bottom of the controller completely and evenly with heatsink grease before mounting it on the plate.

This plate needs to be positioned in the airflow for cooling. On our Voltsrabbit^{TM}, I made a slight bend in one edge of the plate and mounted it along the passenger side front fender, at an angle from the fender down to a chassis seam. This left airflow behind the plate.

On a Porsche 914, one of our customers installed his controller on standoffs on the firewall behind the driver's seat. The bottom inch of the plate extended under the car into the airstream. In motion, this caught the air and funnelled it up between the plate and the firewall, providing very effective cooling.

Temperature control is the most critical factor in controller performance. If the controller position does not achieve good airflow, duct air to the back of the plate from elsewhere. For a high performance race car, or a car with a rigorous duty cycle including long steep hills, use a finned heatsink plate.

All of these controllers are for DC motor systems. The AC motor needs an entirely different controller. An AC controller needs to be, in effect, three DC controllers synchronized together. For this reason, it is also very expensive and bulky, and not generally used by hobbyists.

The other part of the speed control system is the potbox, or potentiometer. This device is connected to the throttle pedal. It is typically a 0 - 5 kohm unit much like a dimmer knob on a light switch. Depending on how much the throttle is depressed, it sends a resistance signal ranging from 0 - 5 kohm to the controller. The controller interprets this signal and varies the duration of the energy pulses proportionately. The following remarks relate specifically to the Curtis/PMC potbox, since it is the most widely used.

The potbox must be mounted rigidly to be effective. Adjusting the throttle linkage is one of the trickiest and most critical operations for good performance. This is the time to review your notes on the original throttle linkage and its travel distances. If the potbox does not

"Temperature control is the most critical factor for controller performance."

achieve full 'on', the car will never have full performance.

If it does not achieve full 'off' position, there are other problems. The PMC potbox has a high-pedal lockout safety feature. This means that the controller will not operate if you try to start the car with a partially depressed throttle. This is to protect against an abrupt and unexpected lurch when the car is turned on. Therefore, if the potbox cannot return to the full 'off' position, the car can't be started.

In the Voltsrabbit™, the potbox uses the original cable for the throttle, part of the original bracket for the cable, and an auxiliary throttle return spring.

Although the potbox has its own return spring, a second spring should be used as well to insure that the lever returns to the full 'off' position when released.

The potbox lever arm has several holes spaced along it for the throttle linkage, to allow different travel distances. If none of the existing holes works for your throttle, you can build an extension for the arm and add more holes.

On one car I built (a Plymouth Arrow) I was able to install the potbox on the firewall directly above the throttle pedal, with a piece of the original linkage fitting into one of the potbox arm holes. You will rarely get this lucky.

On the Voltsrabbit™, I mounted it on the passenger side shock tower, and used the original diesel throttle cable, along with a couple of pieces adapted from the original fuel injection linkage. You will have to experiment with the best location, mounting bracket, and linkage for your car. Take the time to be precise in this operation, and it will serve you well later.

Incidentally, the potbox contains the first of five emergency disconnects that should be in the system. This is a microswitch that functions as a 'deadman' switch. Any time the throttle is released, the microswitch opens the main contactor, shutting off all power to the controller.

Main Contactor

The main contactor is the second emergency disconnect. This contactor allows you to turn the system on and off with an ignition key, just like a gas car. The main contactor should be mounted as close as possible to the terminals of the controller, since they will be connected.

Some people have tried to eliminate the contactor and, in effect, leave the car 'on' all the time. After all, there isn't any electricity flowing when the car is standing still, and you still have the circuit breaker, right?

Wrong. In most layouts, the circuit breaker must be closed during charging. This leaves the components vulnerable to the incoming electricity. I know of one man whose controller overheated during charging, started a fire, and nearly burned down his garage—all because he decided he didn't need a main contactor.

A main contactor, with a diode to suppress voltage spikes.

Cheap contactors can fail, and may fail in a closed (full on) position. Use a contactor that is intended for use in an electric vehicle. The Albright seems to be the most widely used. It will withstand repeated openings and closings without wear, since it is never opening or closing under load. It includes a magnetic blow-out feature to suppress arcing at the contacts.

It is also advisable to install a diode across the small terminals on the positive side of the contactor, to protect the 12-volt electrical system from the voltage spikes generated by turning the contactor off. The band on the diode should be toward the top of the contactor, where the large terminals are.

Since the contactor can produce a spark, it should be mounted below the level of the battery tops. That way, any potentially explosive hydrogen will rise away from the contactor.

Page 69

Circuit Breaker

The third emergency disconnect is a circuit breaker. As I mentioned earlier, this should be installed between the battery pack and the main contactor, or between any two batteries in the circuit. The breaker operates in two ways. In case of a problem involving excessive current draw, the breaker will flip automatically and shut down the system. However, it can also be flipped manually if you suspect a problem, or if you simply want to disable the system for safety while the car is parked, displayed, or being worked on.

For manual operation, the breaker must be mounted so the driver can reach it. Ideally, this means in or under the dash. I mount mine so the 'on' position is toward the passenger side. In an emergency, a simple swipe of the hand toward me will flip it off.

A DC circuit breaker.

Another location could be near the floor beside the driver's seat. If it is necessary to mount the breaker outside the passenger compartment, it can be cable-actuated by a pull inside the car. I have done this with a knob installed on the firewall, and one customer used the bright red heater lever in his Porsche 914.

Be careful that the breaker is not mounted where it will be accidentally tripped by a foot or knee.

If the breaker is installed in a remote location, it will be inconvenient to get out of the car and reset it. However, if something caused the breaker to trip, you should pull over and determine the cause before continuing anyway.

Although the car will pull several hundred amps of current momentarily under acceleration, the breaker need not be rated that high. A 250-amp breaker with a built-in delay curve will withstand 400-amp draws for five minutes, which is more than adequate. This delay prevents nuisance trips due to non-harmful momentary surges.

The breaker MUST be a DC breaker, not an AC unit. The performance characteristics are different, and an AC breaker will not give you the same kind of protection.

Page 70

Fusible Links

The fourth emergency disconnect in the system is the fusible link. One of these should be mounted in the battery series. If the total pack is split, I recommend a link in each portion.

The link mounts between any two batteries and serves as an interconnect for those two batteries. In case of a short across the pack, such as a dropped tool, or (in the case of a serious collision) chassis sheet metal, the fusible link will blow and open the circuit, disarming the high voltage system.

The link blows by melting apart. It can't be reset like a circuit breaker, but must be replaced. I recommend using a fusible link with a delay, similar to the circuit breaker, to prevent nuisance blows from momentary surges.

A bare fusible link, and one mounted on a plexiglass block in a battery interconnect.

I mount the link on a plexiglass block to give it some additional rigidity. When space permits, I also enclose it in a plex tube to contain any hot lead splatter should the link blow. In an enclosed box, this isn't always possible.

And the fifth emergency disconnect? A good pair of cable shears. If all else fails, cut a cable.

Gauges

You will want to add various gauges to the car. The early EVs often used home-modified panel meters. There are several problems with this kind of gauge. I don't like them because they don't look like they belong in a car.

In fact, they don't. A panel meter is intended to work on stationary equipment inside buildings. It is not built for the vibration, heat, dust, etc. of a vehicle traveling down a road. Heat from the sun will loosen the face and warp it, causing the needle to stick. Road vibrations will damage the delicate mechanism. Dust will work its way inside.

Page 71

Also, panel meters are not backlit for night use.

In a futuristic car like an EV, there is a tendency to go for digital instruments. If you are a real techie, a digital gauge can give you all the precision and detail your heart desires. However, these also have drawbacks.

One problem is lighting. Both LEDs and LCDs are hard or impossible to read in full sunlight. LCDs are not lit for night use.

A second problem has to do with constant fluctuations. The EV system in motion is continuously changing its voltage and amperage readings. Under acceleration and deceleration, the numbers may change so quickly that it is impossible to get a sensible reading from a digital gauge.

A third problem is psychological. It requires more concentration to read a number and interpret its meaning than to glance at the position of a needle. The two operations use different parts of the brain. The second one can be done much more quickly and automatically.

An LED bar gauge (top), panel meters (center), round automotive-style gauges (bottom left), and a digital gauge (bottom right). Note how the face on the leftmost panel meter is faded from the sun.

For these reasons, I prefer standard automotive-style (and quality) round analog gauges. I find them to be accurate, readable, durable, and attractive.

I also discovered a critical visibility factor in these round gauges. Traditional round automotive gauges are designed and built to be installed in the dash at the factory, more or less in the direct line of sight of the driver. In a conversion, however, the dash is often fully occupied already by the speedometer, clock, and other original gauges, and would be very hard to modify. This means that the EV gauges are often mounted to the right and down, even possibly on a console.

On a conventional round gauge, this can mean that the numbers along the top of the face are hidden behind the bezel of the gauge.

There are two solutions to this problem. One is to fabricate a mount that sits at an angle to correct the line of sight for the driver.

I took the other solution. I contracted with my

gauge manufacturer to build gauges upside-down. That is, the face is located on the bottom half of the circle with the numbers reversed so they still read correctly, and the needle still sweeps from left to right.

Another advantage to standard round automotive gauges is that there are numerous attractive mounts available for them at parts stores.

The gauge you will use most will be the ammeter. There is no real corollary to this in a gas car. This is an efficiency gauge. Moment by moment, it tells you how much energy you are using. The scale will go from 0 to 400 or 550 amps. At the end of this book, once your car is built, we'll talk about how to use the information given to you by this gauge and others.

The gauge you will use next most often will be a voltmeter showing your traction pack voltage. This gauge can come in two forms. The first is a straight numbered voltmeter. This will give you precise voltage information, and you will need to know what those numbers mean for your particular system and vehicle.

The gauge may read from 0 to 100 or 150 volts. However, it isn't necessary to go all the way to 0, since a typical controller cuts out at 45 volts. An expanded scale gauge that starts at 50 will give you more detail in a useful range. You also want to be sure the gauge reads high enough. A fully charged system is actually about 8.3% higher than its nominal voltage, so a fully charged 96 volt system will read about 104 volts.

The main use for the voltmeter is as a 'fuel gauge'. If you're not really interested in the precise numbers, but just want to know how much 'fuel' you have left, you can get this gauge in the other form: as a fuel gauge.

The simplest type, which I prefer, is an expanded scale voltmeter labelled in percentages, from 0 to 100%. The batteries are considered 'drained' at 80% of full charge, so only the top 20% of charge is actually usable. This kind of gauge measures only that usable portion. I find it very accurate and easy to use.

There are other fuel gauges that do the same thing with a segmented LED bar. Although some people prefer them, I do not. They tend to be more expensive, and less precise, since the bar only has about eight segments to light up, rather than a continuous needle sweep.

These LED bar gauges are sampling voltmeters. Since voltage varies constantly with acceleration, these gauges sample the voltage over a period of seconds and display an average. Some of them have a peculiarity: they can be fooled into reading too low. If you are drawing down the voltage for an extended time (as when climbing a long hill), the gauge will show an artificially low voltage. When you reach flat ground again, you are not drawing as hard on the batteries, and the voltage comes back up. However, some gauges will not reset upward. They move down only, one notch at a time, and reset to 'full' only when the car is plugged in and fully recharged.

Another type of fuel gauge is a watt-hour meter. This gauge ignores the amount of electricity in the batteries. It only measures flow: what goes in and what comes out. It is necessary to calibrate the watt-hour meter for a specific battery pack and vehicle. A 'zero' point must be arbitrarily chosen and set. Since an EV

"A fully charged system is actually about 8.3% higher than its nominal voltage."

does not run out of fuel abruptly, but simply goes slower and slower, you must choose the point at which you consider the batteries 'drained'. You will also have to experiment to determine what constitutes 'full' for your car.

Once that is done, the watt-hour meter will measure the electricity as it goes into and out of the batteries, and display a 'current balance'.

This kind of instrument can give a great deal of detailed information for those interested in technical details or diagnostics. However, it isn't cheap, and does require a certain amount of calibration and periodic recalibration. This is an instrument more for the serious EV enthusiast than for the casual driver.

After the fuel gauge or voltmeter for the high voltage system, a third type of gauge you may want is a voltmeter for the 12-volt system. This typically reads from 6 to 16 volts, and reports on the condition of the auxiliary battery that powers the lights, wipers, etc. This gauge is optional if the car has a DC/DC converter, but it's still nice to have if there's room for it.

Automotive-style gauges, built 'upside-down' for better visibility, and the shunt for the ammeter.

A fourth type of gauge is a tachometer. This is very nice to have, but is a little more complicated to install. In an EV, since there are no spark plugs, common gas car tachs won't work. It is necessary to use a magnetic or optical sensor to count either the teeth on the flywheel or protrusions on a plate mounted on a second shaft at the rear of the motor. The tach must be calibrated to match the sensor.

If you are lucky, you may have some round gauge you no longer need (such as oil pressure) which you can replace with an EV gauge. If you are really adventurous, you can try to install gauges in unused areas of the original gauge cluster behind the steering wheel, but I don't recommend it. The space behind the dash is tight, full of wires, and difficult to work in. In newer cars, much of the circuitry is built into the dash itself as a printed circuit board. You are likely to cause yourself much grief.

Sturdy and attractive gauge mounts are commercially available for standard round gauges. These usually mount on top of the dash. You may also be able to fabricate a mounting plate to fit into a blank or unneeded part of the central dash area, such as below or above the radio, or in place of a coin tray. Lower down in a central console may be another possibility.

The primary consideration for gauge placement should be visibility for the driver. The gauge should be as close to eye level as possible. Sometimes this isn't possible. Give placement priority first to the ammeter, then to the tach if you have one, then to the fuel gauge, and last to the low voltage gauge.

Check that the gauge numbers and needle are easily visible, not just the flat face, and check it in full sunlight if possible. Slight changes in angle can sometimes make a big difference.

Plan your gauge mounts so that wires can be collected tidily out of sight and danger. Choose locations where the driver will not be continually bumping the gauge with arms or knees.

The dash of a late model Voltsrabbit™, showing an ammeter and state-of-charge gauge, and the circuit breaker at the bottom.

Shunt

We mentioned the shunt briefly when we were talking about the controller, but I want to explain it a little more fully here.

The shunt is necessary for the ammeter. Without it, you would have to run 2/0 cable up under the dash to your gauge. The shunt gets around this by converting the current passing through it to a calibrated millivolt signal. This signal can be routed to the gauge on very small wires. The ammeter is, in fact, a millivolt meter that has been calibrated to match the shunt and display in amps.

The shunt can be mounted anywhere, but since you don't want to run cable any further than necessary, it is best to mount it close to the action, by the controller. This is why it works out so well when mounted on the component plate.

When we get to the section on wiring, we'll talk about how to hook up the gauges to collect information from different parts of the system.

DC/DC Converter

When we were talking about gauges, we mentioned a DC/DC converter. This is an electronic device that takes the place of the alternator in a gas car.

The electric car still needs a source of 12 volts to operate the lights, horn, and some of the EV components. It isn't a good idea to tap off the first two batteries in the pack to get this voltage, because those batteries will discharge more than the others. An unevenly charged pack will not perform as well. When charging, the rest of the batteries will be overcharged and gassing, which is not good for them, while the charger is still working to bring the two low ones up and equalize them. This will shorten the lives of the batteries. Finally, some components need a source of 12 volts that is grounded to the chassis. The traction batteries MUST NOT be grounded to the chassis.

A DC/DC converter.

For all these reasons, you need a 12-volt auxiliary battery. However, the electric car no longer has an alternator to keep this battery charged. You could add one, but it would use up horsepower that is better used to move the car.

The early EVs ran a 'total loss' 12-volt system. This means the 12-volt battery got charged at the same time as the others, and then was gradually drained while the car was driven. This was a less than optimum situation. A normal car battery couldn't take that kind of abuse, so it was necessary to use a heavy-duty deep cycle marine battery. Even so, it didn't take long, when using the lights or wipers, to start draining the battery.

Then the lights would grow dim, and the wipers and turn signals would cycle more and more slowly.

A DC/DC converter taps off the entire battery pack at a very low amperage. This means that all the batteries are discharged evenly, and the current draw is negligible. Typically, on a 96-volt system, it is only drawing about 6 amps. It converts this to a regulated output of 13.5 volts at 25 amps and charges the auxiliary battery continuously. The converter is internally isolated, so the high voltage and low voltage systems never connect directly.

This not only maintains bright lights and brisk wipers, but it allows you to use a very small 12-volt starting battery for your auxiliary battery. You do still need some kind of battery. The converter itself requires a source of 12 volts to turn it on. Also, the converter cuts out at 72 volts or less. Under a heavy load, as when climbing a steep hill, it is possible to pull your battery pack momentarily below 72 volts. If this should happen at night and you had no auxiliary battery, you would suddenly be without lights. Finally, if the converter should fail for some reason, and you had no auxiliary battery, you would be stuck where you were. With a battery, you will certainly have at least enough power to get home.

All DC/DC converters are not created equal. If you shop around, you will find vast price differences. The difference is the same as the difference between panel meters and automotive gauges. Many DC/DC converters are used for electronic equipment such as computers, in stationary climate-controlled conditions. Others were designed for the rigors of industrial EVs. You want the second kind for your car.

Chargers

Early charging systems were very crude, and hard on the batteries. Some simply slugged current into the batteries until an arbitrarily-set timer turned them off. Others permitted their current to be adjusted down as the battery charge came up, but required a lot of attention and adjusting during the charging cycle. And those adjustments were still just the operator's best guess.

The result was that batteries were charged too hard or too long, and they bubbled and gassed a lot. Besides smelling bad and making a mess on the battery tops, this also shortened battery life.

Then came 'smart' chargers. These were able to sense the battery pack's state of charge, and automatically adjust the current downward in increments. Some were smart enough to turn themselves off when the car was fully charged, and even turn back on if the car sat unused long enough for the charge to start to fall off. Others simply tapered to a low-level finish charge to equalize all the batteries.

Until recently chargers were bigger than a breadbox, and weighed 70 - 100 pounds. These were usually not mounted on the car, but kept in the garage. The bulk and weight were due to the transformers used inside the chargers.

Now we have chargers the size of a toaster that

"Now we have chargers the size of a toaster, and weighing 10 pounds."

weigh 10 pounds. They have achieved this weight loss by eliminating the large transformers. In doing this, they also sacrificed the safety feature of isolating the current internally. To compensate, they have incorporated a ground fault interrupter. This will trip instantly, much like a circuit breaker, if it detects an improperly grounded circuit that could pose a safety hazard.

The smaller chargers are quickly taking over the market, much as PWM controllers took over from SCRs. They are compact enough to mount on the car, opening up opportunities for charging at destinations rather than just at home base.

A major consideration when choosing a charger is the input voltage. There are trade-offs between 110 volts and 220 volts. The 110-volt option is very popular because it is so readily available for opportunity charging away from home. The disadvantage is a long charge time—10 - 12 hours for a completely depleted pack. This is no problem overnight at home, but it does mean that two hours of charging at a friend's house won't bring the pack up a lot.

A 220-volt system can charge a depleted pack in 6 - 8 hours. However, 220-volt outlets are not as readily available.

A 110-volt input charger, (bottom left), a booster unit (top left) for charging a pack of 114 volts or more with the 110-volt input charger, and a 220-volt input charger (right).

In the past, it has usually been necessary to choose one input voltage or the other. The 110-volt system had a further advantage because it was the first to come out in the smaller, compact version.

Now, compact 220-volt chargers are becoming available, and even compact chargers that can accept either input voltage. There are also devices being developed and introduced to 'pulse' the charging current, allowing batteries to be charged much faster. Chargers are likely to evolve quickly in the next few years.

In addition, you must consider the output voltage. Some chargers come preset for one size of battery pack, and cannot be adjusted. If you decide to increase the size of your battery pack, you will need to get a new charger. Others offer options, and can be adjusted internally for various battery pack voltages.

I do not recommend home-built chargers. They will sacrifice safety, or battery life, or both.

You will have to choose the charger that best suits your needs. Always buy something that is actually in production from a real manufacturer, is packaged in a sturdy case, has some kind of ground fault interrupter or similar protection, and provides an automatically tapering charge based on battery pack charge level. Beyond those constants, ask the following questions:

1. How big is it and how much does it weigh?
2. What input voltage(s) does it accept?
3. What output voltage(s) does it provide?
4. How fast will it charge my car?

Inverters

If you were using an AC system, you would also need and inverter to change the DC electricity in the batteries into AC electricity for the motor to use. Since AC systems are not generally used by the individual enthusiast, I won't go into more detail about inverters here.

Power Brake Vacuum System

If your donor car has power brakes, you definitely want to keep them. The converted EV will be heavier, and needs all the braking it can get. The original power brake unit used vacuum from the manifold to operate it. Since you no longer have a manifold, you will have to provide another source of vacuum.

This can be done easily with a small 12-volt electric vacuum pump, a reservoir, and a vacuum switch. Most power brake units require about 14 inches of vacuum. I use a switch that kicks on when vacuum drops to 17 inches. A reservoir can be built easily from an 8"

A power brake vacuum system, including pump, reservoir, switch, and brass fittings.

length of schedule 40 ABS plastic pipe and two pipe caps. (I prefer ABS to PVC for aesthetic reasons: black ABS looks like it 'belongs', and white PVC always looks scuffed.) Be sure the hose you use is actual power brake hose. A diode should also be installed in the circuit to protect the vacuum switch.

There are various vacuum pumps available. I shopped around until I found one that was fairly compact, relatively quiet, and could pull down the vacuum within 9 seconds. The reservoir and switch will allow you a few normal applications of the brakes, after which the pump will come on briefly to restore vacuum.

If you have an older VW with front drum brakes, you might want to refit it with discs. If your donor does not come with power brakes, you might want to see if there were other versions of the same (or similar) models that did have power brakes, find one in a junkyard, and retrofit the system to your car. You can also often upgrade the existing brakes with heavier-duty shoes or pads.

Component Mounts

Each mount for each car will be different, the product of your ingenuity. I recommend first examining original mounts that you removed with the IC components. There may be something there that you can modify slightly and re-use.

Locate your components for easy accessibility. Build your mounts so they will be secure, and not twist or oscillate under normal driving conditions. Use nuts and bolts instead of sheet metal screws for added security.

The layout of the components and design and fabrication of the mounts is the part of the conversion where you can best express your creativity and design talent. Attention to detail in this area is the key that separates a really awful conversion from an adequate one, and an adequate one from a professional-quality conversion.

10 Wiring

Once all the components are physically mounted in the car, it's time to wire them up. I'll separate this task into low current wiring and high current wiring, although some of the low current wires actually carry high voltage. Essentially, this means small gauge wires vs. heavy cables.

Using too small a gauge of wire will cause inefficient operation, and possibly a fire. Wires can become very hot in use if they are undersized for the current they are carrying.

The gauge of wire needed is determined by watts of electricity and length of the wire. The higher the wattage or longer the wire, the larger the gauge needs to be. You can determine the wattage by multiplying the volts times the amps for the particular component you are wiring. Most of the small gauge wiring will be 16-gauge, but some may be as large as 10-gauge. (Perversely, the larger the gauge number of the wire, the smaller the wire. This means 10-gauge is much bigger than 16-gauge.)

High current wiring should be 2/0 cable. I like to use welding cable. This has finer strands of copper than ordinary 2/0 cable, which makes it much more flexible. It also has much heavier insulation.

Regular 2/0 cable, and welding cable.

Let's lay out some general principles that apply to both kinds of wiring. Wires need to be protected from cuts, abrasion, snagging, and tension. For this reason, they need to be secured close to the chassis at frequent intervals (so they won't catch on anything) but they should never be stretched tight.

They should not press against any corners of the components or chassis, not even gently rounded corners. In time, normal vibrations can cause that corner to abrade through the insulation and cause a short.

Page 81

WIRE GAUGE CHART

Load In Watts	Length Of Wire Run In Feet											
	3'	5'	7'	10'	15'	20'	25'	30'	40'	50'	75'	100'
12	18	18	18	18	18	18	18	18	18	18	18	18
18	18	18	18	18	18	18	18	18	18	18	18	18
24	18	18	18	18	18	18	18	18	18	18	16	16
36	18	18	18	18	18	18	18	18	18	18	14	14
48	18	18	18	18	18	18	18	18	18	16	12	12
60	18	18	18	18	18	18	18	18	16	14	12	12
72	18	18	18	18	18	18	16	16	16	14	12	10
84	18	18	18	18	18	18	16	16	14	14	10	10
96	18	18	18	18	18	16	16	16	14	12	10	10
120	18	18	18	18	16	16	16	14	12	12	12	10
132	18	18	18	18	16	16	14	14	12	12	10	8
144	18	18	18	18	16	16	14	14	12	12	10	8
180	18	18	18	18	14	14	12	12	12	10	8	8
216	18	18	16	16	14	14	12	12	10	10	8	8
240	18	18	16	16	14	12	10	10	10	10	8	6
264	18	18	16	16	12	12	10	10	10	8	6	6
288	18	18	16	16	12	12	10	10	10	8	6	6
360	18	16	16	14	10	10	10	10	10	6	4	4
480	18	16	14	12	10	10	8	8	6	6	4	2
600	16	14	12	12	10	10	8	8	6	6	2	2
1200	12	12	10	10	6	6	4	4	4	2	1	0
1800	10	10	8	8	4	4	2	2	2	1	00	00
2400	10	8	8	6	4	4	2	2	1	0	4/0	4/0

Obviously, it's even more important to protect wires from sharp edges that could cut them. Whenever a wire must pass through a hole cut in sheet metal, it should be protected by a grommet. If you can't find a grommet to fit the hole, it's easy to make one. Cut a short piece of hose, such as VW fuel line. This is a type of rubber hose with a braided cloth surface. Slit the hose lengthwise, and cut it to fit the hole so that the hose curls into a donut shape, with the slit along the outside edge to receive the edge of the sheet metal. Glue it into place with automotive trim cement.

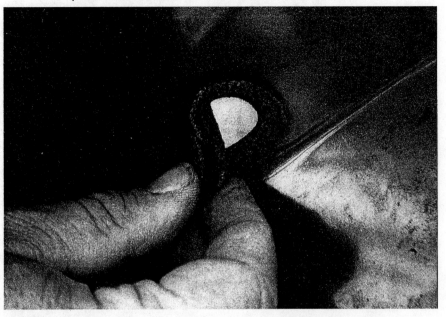

A grommet made from VW fuel line.

Loose connections are a source of electrical resistance. Resistance means poor performance, corrosion, heat, and fire hazard. Always be sure that any wiring crimps or connections are secure.

Identifying wires is important. This is usually done by color codes and a wiring diagram. You will be using some of the car's original wiring for new purposes. Any time you need to extend an original wire, try to match the original color code as closely as possible. Many wires have a base color and a contrasting stripe. Match your new wire to the base color, and mark it periodically (at least near any connections) with model paint or touch-up paint that matches the original stripe. If for some reason you have to change a wire color, record the location and color change in your Project Notebook.

Likewise, when you add new wires, develop your own color code and diagram for them in your Project Notebook. Nothing is worse than a vehicle all prettily wired with a single color of wire! You can make things easier by following established protocols in your original shop manual: this color is always ground, etc.

Installing Front-To-Rear Wiring

This topic includes both high and low current wiring. In most cars, the battery pack is split between the front and the rear of the car, and it is necessary to run small gauge wires and two large cables between the two areas. This is most easily done if the cables and wires are gathered together and installed all at once.

There is another reason to run the two cables together as well. Running them side-by-side will minimize any high-frequency electrical noise from the controller which might interfere with your radio.

You want to install the wires and cables where they will be protected from road hazards. Some cars may offer a built-in protected wiring channel. For instance, my customer with the Porsche 914 used the heater tube.

If you are running the cables and wires beneath the car, they will need added protection. I like to use PVC flexible hose, which is also called 'spa hose'. It is available in various diameters. I use the 1 1/2" diameter hose, which is just barely wide enough for a pair of 2/0 cables. A little later I'll explain how to feed the cables through the hose. Before you work with this hose, it helps to let it lie in the sun for a while to soften up and 'relax'.

Check the underside of the car for a likely path for this hose. There may be an appropriate route where the fuel lines or exhaust system were removed. There may even be brackets in place that you can adapt. If so, this is where the carefully labelled baggies of hardware you removed will come in handy.

If there is nothing usable in place, it's easy to fabricate a few L-shaped metal brackets with a hole in one side of the 'L' and a slot in the other, just at the corner. These can be pop-riveted to the chassis at intervals, and the hose secured to them with hose clamps.

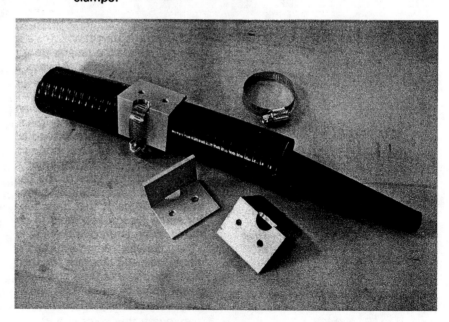

Cables in a PVC hose sheath, with mounting brackets.

Once you've determined how and where you will run this front-to-rear bundle of wiring, you need to figure out exactly how much of which kind of wire you need.

For small gauge wiring, count how many wires you will need, then add two to four extras. That way, if you decide to add some other component or gauge at a later date, you will already have usable wires in place. Record the colors of these spare wires in your Project Notebook.

Four-in-one trailer wire is very handy for this kind of front-to-rear small gauge wiring. This is a ribbon consisting of four color-coded 16-gauge wires lightly joined together at the edges. It makes a tidy ready-made loom for running the length of the car. At each end, you can peel the individual wires away from the ribbon one at a time to route them to the appropriate components.

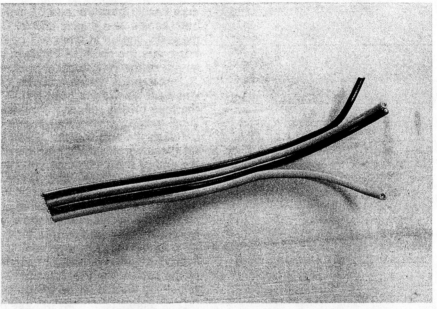

Four-in-one trailer wire makes a tidy ready-made loom.

When running small gauge wires front-to-rear, use 1 1/2 times the length of the car in wire. That will give you enough slack for all the ups and downs and twists and turns between the start and finish. You will have a little extra wire to cut off at each end, but you won't come up short.

To measure cable, you need to be more precise. If you are using PVC hose, fasten it temporarily in position. Take a 6' length of rope about the same diameter as the cable and fasten it to the very end of the PVC hose in the front of the car. Then lay it along your intended cable route to the destination of the front end of the positive cable. Mark the cable at this point and label the mark with a masking tape flag as 'F+'. Do the same thing for the front negative cable. Move the rope to the rear of the car and repeat the procedure for the two rear ends of the cables.

To determine the length of the positive cable, measure the rope from the PVC hose end to the 'F+' mark, and from the PVC hose end to the 'R+' mark. Add those two measurements together, and add the total to the length of the PVC hose itself. Then add 6" to each end to give you some extra slack. Do the same calculations for the negative cable, and cut both cables to suit.

Now it's time to feed the cables and wires into the PVC hose. I call this 'feeding the snake' because it's kind of like force-feeding an uncooperative boa constrictor. Take the cable that extends farthest into the engine compartment and crimp a lug onto the end. (See crimping instructions on page 95.) Mark the end of the cable next to the lug with masking tape and an 'F+' or 'F-', as appropriate. Measure back the distance you marked on your rope, add the 6" of slack, and mark the cable with a crayon or tape. This mark indicates where the cable should emerge from the PVC hose.

Without crimping on the lug, do the same labelling, measurement and marking, including the 6" of slack, for the other cable. Lay the two cables out side by side on the floor, with the marks lined up. Do the same procedure (label, measure, add 6" and mark) on the far ends of both cables as a double check. These marks should automatically line up at what will be the far end of the PVC hose, and the distance between the marks should be the length of the PVC hose.

Wrap the cables together with a single turn of electrical tape at the front PVC hose mark, but don't cut the tape off the roll yet. Now you want to nestle any small gauge wires or four-in-one ribbon into the trough between the two cables. If you know approximately how far these wires extend into the engine compartment from the end of the PVC hose, you can measure them and align them with the hose mark. If not, split the difference so that about the same amount of wire extends on each end of the PVC hose. Once the wires are measured and nestled against the cables, secure them with another wrap of electrical tape, then cut the tape.

Depending on how many small gauge wires you are including, you may want to secure one or more on one side of the cables, flip the assembly over, and secure the remaining wire(s) in the trough on the other side. Use only the minimal amount of tape necessary, as too much tape will make it hard to pass the cables through the hose.

Align the cables and wires neatly and secure them with a single loop of tape at approximately 2' intervals, and at the rear PVC hose mark. At the front end, tape all the cables and wires together wherever one of the shorter cables or wires ends, so it will not try to fold back when going through the hose.

You'll need to lubricate the cable bundle to slide it into the hose. There are a couple of ways this can be done. One way is to start spraying silicon lubricant into one end of the PVC hose while constantly rotating the hose, and keep spraying until it starts to run out the far end. Then you feed the cables into it, as I am about to describe.

The second method is to lube the cables as they are fed in, using electrician's wire-pulling lubricant (also known as 'slime').

In either case, remove the PVC hose from the car and secure one end in a bench vise. Run a length of mechanic's wire through the hose so that about 2' of it sticks out at each end. Take the wire at the end opposite the vise and thread it through the lug on the end of the longest front cable. Then wrap it around itself several times, thread it back through the lug the other way, and wrap it around itself again.

The silicone spray method can be done by one person pulling on the mechanic's wire at the vise. The slime method requires at least two people: one to pull, and another to slime and feed the cable, with room for other participants to steady the center section or assist at either end. This method usually produces a great deal of hilarity in all involved before it is finished.

The person pulling the cables at the vise end should wear heavy leather work gloves to keep the mechanic's wire from cutting into the skin. Once the lug emerges, a screwdriver can be inserted in the lug up to the hilt and used as a two-handed handle for pulling.

If you are using the slime, buy the smallest bottle possible, because you won't need more than 1/2 cup. The person at the feeding end should lube the inside of the end of the hose, and the outside edges of both cables. There is no need to lube the flat sides of the bundles. Synchronize pushing the lubed cable into one end of the hose with pulling on the other.

When the front crayon/tape mark reaches the end of the hose, you're done. Double check that the rear mark is also at its end of the hose. Crimp lugs onto the remaining three cable ends now—it's much easier to do on the bench than in the car. Then install the assembly in its permanent position in the car.

Low Current Wiring

There are three fundamental principles to good wiring. We already talked about documentation using color codes and diagrams. The second principle is loom building. Don't run individual wires in all directions. This is what I call the 'explosion in a spaghetti factory' effect. Instead, choose a route that will be appropriate for several wires, and gather them together into a loom, peeling each wire out to its destination as needed. This makes a tidier, more professional conversion, and also makes the car less prone to wiring failures, and easier to work on.

A loom can be gathered in several ways. The wires can merely be tie-wrapped together at intervals, or banded neatly with electrical tape. Sometimes you can follow the path of the original factory loom and secure your loom to it.

There are also a couple of types of wiring loom sheaths available commercially. One is called spiral wrap. As the name implies, it is a spiral that is wrapped around the loom. Individual wires can be fished out between the loops of the spiral.

Another type is called Flex-guard. This is a flexible accordion plastic tube with a slit down its length. The loom is poked into the the tube through the slit, and individual wires are pulled out where needed. The tube is then secured periodically with tie wraps, and there are special caps for the ends. This makes a very clean-looking loom.

If you are really brave, you can encase your loom in shrink tube. This is a thin flexible tube that shrinks to fit when heated. You'd better be absolutely sure that your loom is just the way you want it, because shrink tubes, like diamonds, are forever. Once it is shrunk into place, the only way to get into the loom is to cut the shrink tube off. Even before shrinking, it is not

"A loom makes a tidier, more professional conversion, and also makes the car less prone to wiring failures."

easy to separate a single wire from the loom to direct it elsewhere. Shrink tube is most appropriate on very short runs of wire.

The third principle is good connections. Most electrical failures on gas or electric cars come from poor connections. Two bare wires twisted together and taped over do not constitute a good connection. Use the right size of automotive crimp connector for the wire you are using. They are color coded for wire size: red for 22 - 18 gauge wire, blue for 16 - 14 gauge wire, and yellow for 12 - 10 gauge wire.

Connectors come in varying qualities, so get good ones. I prefer the ones with nylon insulation. It gives a good crimp without cracking. Also, use a good quality crimping tool. Cheap ones will loosen at the hinge pin, and give poor crimps.

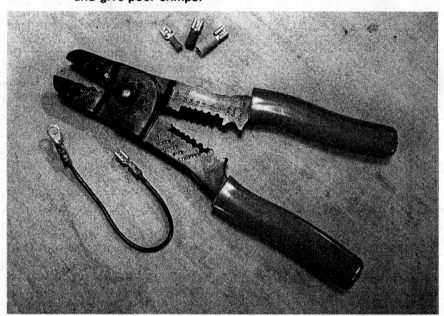

A good quality crimping tool will give you secure connections.

To crimp a connector, strip the insulation from the wire about 1/4" from the end without cutting the wire. A good crimping tool will have calibrated stripping notches for different sizes of wire. If you strip too little insulation, you won't get a good crimp. If you strip too much, you will have bare wire exposed and vulnerable outside the connector.

Slide the wire into the connector. Be sure you are crimping the metal part of the connector, not just the insulating sleeve. Squeeze first with the flat jaws of the crimping tool, then again using the crimping stud to leave a distinctive dimple in the connector. Finally, give the connector a good hard tug to test the crimp.

I have never had a failure from a properly crimped connector. I do not believe in soldering these connections, for several reasons. One is that crimp-on connectors are also called 'solderless' connectors. God intended them to work just fine without solder, so why waste your time?

Another reason is that soldering is messy and dangerous. Finally, a poorly soldered connection will be worse than one that was not soldered at all.

Page 88

**"It is important
to keep the
12-volt accessory
system and the
high voltage
traction system
isolated from
each other."**

There is an occasional exception to this practice. For example, the wires for my gauges are simply too fine to be effectively crimped, so I soldered them.

The 12-volt electrical system for the accessories will ground to the chassis, while the main high voltage traction system will not. It is important to keep these two systems isolated from each other.

When you need to ground something in the 12-volt system, check your shop manual for the location of factory grounds, and use them if possible. On the newer cars, the paint system is such that you cannot get a good ground simply by poking a hole in the sheet metal. If you do need to create a ground, sand the area around the hole down to bare shiny metal.

Most of the car's original wiring will stay intact for things like headlights, wipers, and horns. Other original wires, no longer needed, will be put to new uses. Still other wires will be completely new, added to the car specifically for the conversion.

The first wire you need to locate is the original hot lead from the battery to the fuse block and ignition switch. Be sure that this path was not interrupted by removing the IC components. If it was, restore it. Also confirm that the battery ground to the chassis is still intact.

The original wiring used a heavy #4 wire from the battery positive terminal solely for the high amperage draw of the starter. The converted EV won't need that heavy wire. If the positive battery wire has a lighter weight wire, such as a 10 gauge, or a series of fusible links pigtailed to it, you can cut the #4 wire at the terminal end and tape it off out of the way. The lighter pigtail will serve your needs.

If the original small gauge wire for the accessories came from the positive terminal of the starter, you will need to extend that wire to reach the battery, replacing the heavy positive battery wire. To connect it to the battery, install a universal battery cable terminal on the battery post and a ring connector on the wire. Then bolt the ring connector to the universal terminal.

You should now have power to the original fuse block and ignition switch. Check this with a voltmeter.

Next check the power out of the ignition switch. To do this, find the original wire (under the hood) from the ignition to the coil. This wire should have been marked with a label when it was disconnected in the disassembly stage.

Check the voltage out of this wire with the key turned to the 'on' position, but not all the way to 'start'. If it is somewhere between 0 and 12 volts there may be a resistor in this part of the system. It may be clearly visible on or near the coil, and easy to remove. Otherwise, check your shop manual. Sometimes the wire itself has a built-in resistor. If so, you will need to replace this wire.

All of your accessories will get their 12-volt power from this source. When there are multiple components using the same power source or ground, this is accomplished most neatly by connecting them all through a common terminal block. In this case, we will want to have separate fuses for each component. We could do this with

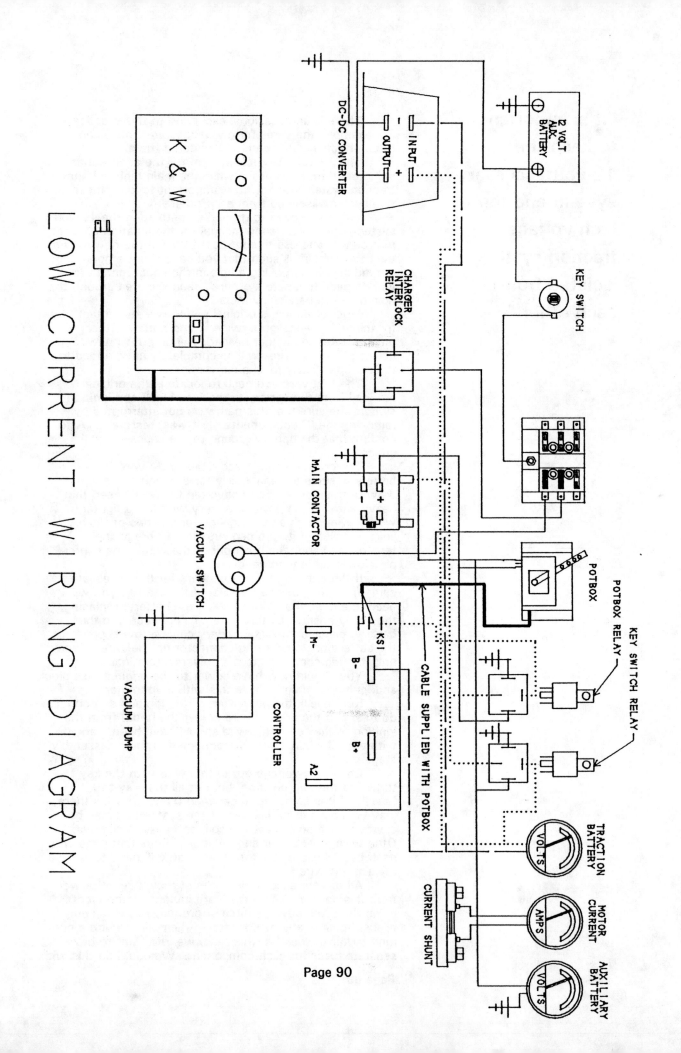

LOW CURRENT WIRING DIAGRAM

Page 90

inline fuses, but the same thing can be done better by using a fuse block instead of an ordinary terminal block. I prefer the type with spade-style fuses. Use fuses rated at double the amperage of the component.

A spade-style fuse block, and two different styles of terminal block, one with a cover.

A little later, we'll be talking about the charger interlock relay. It will fit into the circuit either just before or just after the new fuse block you are adding. Choose which leg of the circuit to put it in based on which will use shorter and more convenient wiring runs.

If you have any components that draw more than 20 amps, wire them directly from the battery using a separate 10 gauge wire, and use a relay to give you ignition key control for these high-load items.

Often you will have two or three components drawing power from the same source. Rather than running individual wires for each, I prefer to start with one wire and 'tap' it as needed along the route to serve the various components. When the wire reaches the first component on the route, I cut it in two and strip both ends. Then I twist the ends together and crimp them both into one appropriate-sized connector. The connector goes to the proper terminal for this component, and the wire continues on to the next. This can be done as many times as needed.

All of your components should come with wiring diagrams or instructions from your supplier. I will give some wiring instructions here for the components most commonly in use.

The Curtis/PMC PB-6 potbox comes with two small wires encased in a grey plastic sheath. These wires need to be connected to the two bottom terminals of the three small terminals on the Curtis/PMC 1221 controller. It doesn't matter which wire goes on which terminal, as long as they use the two bottom ones.

The PB-6 has a safety feature built into it, in the form of a deadman microswitch. When properly wired, this opens the main contactor and cuts off all power to the controller whenever the throttle is fully released. Unfortunately, there are a couple of components you don't want to turn off every time you release the throttle, such as the DC/DC converter and the dash voltmeter or state-of-charge gauge.

To get around this, insert a couple of relays into the circuit to insure that these components bypass the deadman microswitch and continue to receive power as long as the ignition key is on. The relays I use are 40-amp single-pole single-throw normally-open relays with 12-volt pull-down coils. When a 12-volt current is applied to the relay's pull-down coil, it creates an electromagnetic field which pulls an arm closed against a stationary contact and allows another (much higher voltage) current to pass through the relay to components beyond.

The first relay I call the 'keyswitch relay'. Its purpose is to turn on the DC/DC converter and battery pack voltmeter or state-of-charge gauge with the ignition key. Connect the 12-volt wire from the ignition key to the leftmost terminal of the potbox microswitch with a tap, then continue the wire to one of the pull-down coil terminals of the keyswitch relay. If you have an auxiliary 12-volt battery gauge, connect to the keyswitch relay with a tap, then continue the wire to the positive terminal of your gauge. Connect the negative terminal of the gauge to chassis ground.

A wiring loom tap connected to the keyswitch relay.

Connect the other pull-down coil terminal to a good chassis ground. Next, run a wire from the positive large diameter terminal of the main contactor to the movable arm side of the relay. Connect to the relay with a tap, then continue the wire to the same terminal on the second relay, which we'll talk about in more detail in a minute.

This wire will carry full battery pack voltage, but very little amperage, so it can be a 16-gauge wire. Finally, run a wire from the stationary side of the contact to the positive input terminal on the DC/DC converter and the battery pack voltmeter or state-of-charge gauge, using the tap method I described earlier.

The second relay I call the 'potbox relay'. Its purpose is to close the main contactor, allowing battery pack voltage into the controller, and to turn on the controller, allowing voltage out to the motor. If the contactor were to fail in a 'full on' position, this relay would make it possible to turn off the controller.

Connect a wire to the rightmost terminal of the microswitch. This wire will go to the small positive main contactor terminal, and to the pull-down coil of the potbox relay. This can be done with a tap, or by using the same tap technique to create a 'Y' of wire if these two destinations are too far apart. Finally, connect both the small negative terminal of the main contactor and the other side of the potbox relay pull-down coil to chassis grounds.

The movable arm of the potbox relay is already connected to the main contactor by the same wire we used for the keyswitch relay. Connect the stationary side of the relay to the keyswitch input terminal of the controller.

In some cars, like the early diesel VW Rabbits, an extra relay is needed because the wire from the ignition switch is too small to carry the necessary loads. In this case, the fuse block will receive its 12-volt input directly from the battery instead of from the ignition switch. The ignition switch will operate a high-load relay to turn the power to the fuse block on and off.

If this is true for your car, install a third relay, wiring the ignition 12 volts to the pull-down coil as before. Choose a gauge of wire sufficient for the load of your components, and install it between the positive 12-volt auxiliary battery and the movable arm terminal of the relay. Connect the stationary contact terminal of the relay to the fuse block.

So far, the DC/DC converter and the battery pack voltage gauge or state-of-charge gauge are connected only at the battery pack voltage positive input terminal. The negative input terminal for both components should be connected to the battery pack negative terminal of the controller, using a tap.

The DC/DC input wiring only carries 6 amps, so 16-gauge wire is sufficient. The output wiring, however, will carry up to 30 amps, so it should be 10-gauge. The output negative terminal should be wired to chassis ground. The output positive terminal connects to the 12-volt auxiliary battery positive terminal.

The ammeter does not have positive and negative terminals, as such. You will need to refer to the specific instructions for the gauge you buy. However, in general, the ammeter will have two terminals which will be wired to the two small terminals on the shunt. You have a 50/50 chance of wiring it the right way the first time. If, when it's all hooked up, the ammeter wants to run backwards, reverse the two shunt connections.

If your gauges are backlit (and they should be!), now is the time to wire the lights. For each gauge, one lighting wire will go to chassis ground, and the other to a source of 12 volts from the light switch. If possible, the 12 volts should come from a tap into the car's original lighting system, so that the gauge lights can be operated by the same dimmer switch as the rest of the

"You have a 50/50 chance of wiring the ammeter to the shunt the right way the first time."

dash lights.

On our Voltsrabbit™, I tapped into a light for the cigarette lighter. You may be able to tap into the dash light wiring. However, on newer cars the dash itself is a circuit board for the gauges. In that case, you may have to go back to the light switch to pick up your dash light wiring. Consult the wiring diagram in your factory manual.

In addition to the other low current wiring, there are two dash indicators I like to use. The first is a 'key-on' indicator. Since an electric car (when standing still) is perfectly silent, I like to have some visible feedback that the ignition is on.

I use one of the original dash indicator lights that is no longer relevant. I like to use the alternator light, because is shows a battery or some other electrical icon that is appropriate. However, this is usually a red light, which can be disconcerting.

If you wish to have a key-on light, locate the original wire from the alternator light, and connect it to chassis ground. In most cars, the alternator light gets its positive connection from the ignition switch and ground from the alternator. That's why the light comes on briefly when you are starting the car. Once the alternator starts putting out 12 volts, the light is no longer grounded, and goes out. If the alternator fails, the light grounds and comes on.

We are using that principle to have the light grounded all the time, so that it will be on whenever the ignition is turned on. Double check your factory manual to be sure your alternator light works this way before attempting to wire it up.

The second dash indicator I use is the oil pressure light, which I use for a 'motor-overheating' warning. The Advanced D.C. motors come with a built-in temperature sensor, which is a normally open switch. It closes if the field temperature reaches 120° C, at which point your motor is in danger of overheating and damaging itself.

There are two small gauge wires from the motor for this sensor. Attach either one to chassis ground, and the other to the original dash indicator light wire.

Incidentally, I have never seen this light come on, even when racing at Phoenix in temperatures over 100° F, but it's comforting to know that it's there to warn me.

If you have a vacuum pump for power brakes, it should be wired to keyed 12 volts and appropriately fused. The switch goes into the circuit in the positive wire between the keyed ignition and the pump. The pump negative wire should go to chassis ground. To protect the vacuum switch from arcing, a diode should be placed between the positive and negative wires of the pump motor, with the band on the diode toward the positive side.

The charger wiring will vary, depending on whether your charger is onboard or offboard, and whether it uses 110-volt or 220-volt input. A charger with a separate circuit to charge the 12-volt auxiliary battery will require some extra wiring. These chargers are generally older models, and few of them are still in use.

The one common feature in all these configurations is that there will be wires connected to the most nega-

"Since an electric car (when standing still) is perfectly silent, I like to have some visible feedback that the ignition is on."

tive and most positive connections of the battery pack. These wires will run either to an onboard charger, or to a connector for an offboard charger.

I prefer not to connect the charging wires directly to the battery terminals, because I don't like small gauge connections on the posts. However, sometimes this is necessary to avoid extra runs of long wires. Instead, I prefer to connect to the battery negative post on the controller and the battery pack positive terminal on the main contactor. This will not hurt the components during charging.

We'll start by describing an onboard charger, which is probably 110-volt input. Even with an onboard charger, I do not recommend wiring the battery pack directly into the charger. I prefer to use an Anderson connector, which gives me a quick disconnect. An Anderson connector has two identical halves of rigid plastic that snap together to make a connection and maintain proper polarity.

An onboard charger connected by an Anderson connector.

Attach the wires from the battery pack to one half of an Anderson connector. Attach the other half to the charger, as per the manufacturer's instructions.

For the AC input to the charger, we'll start at the wall and work our way in to the charger. You will use an extension cord between a wall socket and a male connection on the car. This cord should match the specifications set by the charger manufacturer. For example, for the K & W BC-20 charger, this means the cord must be no less than a 12 gauge three-wire cord, and no more than 25 feet long. If the cord is too light or too long, it will overheat in use.

On the car, the cord will attach to a male fixture, which can be a cord end or a solid male receptacle. This should be mounted somewhere convenient, yet protected from the weather. A favorite 'cute' location is the original gas fill opening.

Inside the car, wire the white and the black wires from the male fixture to an AC charger interlock relay that is normally closed and opens when AC is applied. As

I mentioned earlier, this relay should be wired to interrupt the 12-volt circuit either just before or just after the new fuse block.

If your batteries are enclosed in boxes, they will need to be ventilated with fans during charging. In this situation, I use a small terminal block for the charging AC input. The AC power comes into the car and goes to the terminal block, then branches to the charger interlock relay, any ventilating fans, and the charger itself. With this arrangement, the fans come on immediately when the AC is plugged in, and stay on until it is unplugged, preventing any potentially dangerous build-up of hydrogen inside the boxes.

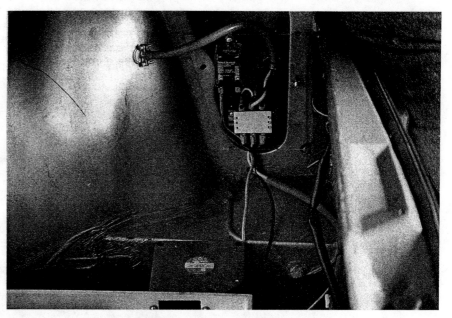

The Voltsrabbit[TM] rear passenger corner, showing battery box vent fan, charger interlock relay, and terminal block.

To wire the AC input into the charger, follow the charger manufacturer's instructions. These will vary from unit to unit.

Also follow the manufacturer's instructions in wiring the DC output from the charger into the second half of the Anderson connector that will send the charge to the battery pack.

If you have an onboard 220-volt input charger, it will be wired almost the same. Of course, you will use wire and extension cord suitable for 220 volts, as specified by the charger manufacturer.

The other difference will occur at the terminal block. While the full 220-volt input goes to the charger, you can split off 110 volts for the interlock relay and ventilating fans.

An offboard charger will almost certainly use 220 volts input. Use an Anderson connector rather than a standard household-style plug to connect the charger to the car. The household plug is not intended to withstand the high current involved. Mount the car's connector in some spot that is convenient to use, yet protected from road splash. Keep in mind that the car will be sitting and charging for several hours at a time, and it is preferable, if possible, not to have to leave a door, hatch, or hood open for charging.

An offboard 220-volt charger complicates the fan and interlock situation, which is another argument in favor of the onboard charger. An interlock can be done in the same manner as we did with the onboard charger. However, a 220-volt relay is more expensive. Also, if your charger has an automatic shut-off, the interlock will also cease to operate when the charger turns off.

The fans are more difficult. It is very hard to find high voltage non-arcing fans. If your charger has a 12-volt output for the auxiliary battery, you can tap into that to run some 12-volt fans as well. If not, you can run a separate 110-volt AC cord to operate the fans and an interlock. This is one more cord strung across your garage and one more step in charging for you to remember. If you are lazy or forgetful, two of your safety features—the fan and the interlock—become non-functional. You could wire a more complex interlock relay system using two relays, so that the charger would not work unless the fans were plugged in. Again, this is one more expense and one more level of complexity.

The moral of the story is: use an onboard charger.

If your charger has a 12-volt output for the auxiliary battery, this will have to be wired in also. Wire this output to the positive terminal of the auxiliary battery and ground it to the chassis, according to the specific instructions of the charger manufacturer.

High Current Wiring

As with low current wiring, solid connections are essential. Cable is generally connected to components by means of lugs on the ends of the cable. It is critical that these lugs are firmly secured to the cable, and protected from corrosion.

I do not recommend soldering lugs to cables. This can be done effectively in manufacturing situations, using special equipment to insure a good, uniform solder joint. However, the chances for success decrease when using home shop equipment. If the temperature is uneven across the area of the solder, you'll get a 'cold joint', which is not a good electrical connection. It will create resistance, inefficiency, and heat.

Even if you get a good joint, there is the possibility of solder wicking up along the copper strands, making the strands rigid and brittle. In manipulating the cable, some of the strands may break and weaken the internal electrical connection.

Finally, soldering something as big as 2/0 cable is an invitation to third degree burns.

It is easy to get a good crimp with a proper crimping tool. One type looks like an enormous pair of vise grips. This works fine (especially if you're interested in building up your arm muscles) but it's expensive. I prefer a small cradle-and-punch type tool. This is a tool manufactured expressly for crimping lugs onto cable. It needs to be used on a solid, flat surface. I put it on top of a square of steel plate on my workbench.

The cradle holds the lug in place, and the punch rides inside a sleeve that keeps it properly aimed. Then you just pound hard on the top of the punch with a ham-

"Soldering something as big as 2/0 cable is an invitation to third degree burns."

mer. There are calibrations on the side of the punch to tell you when you are adequately crimped for 2/0. I just hit it until it won't go any farther.

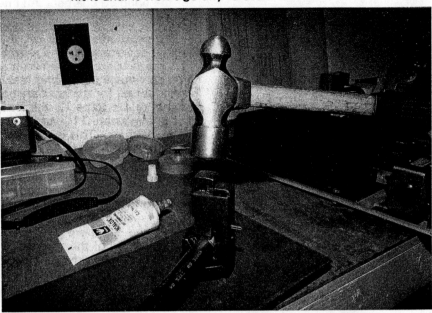

Crimping lugs with a cradle-and-punch style tool.

The entire crimping sequence is as follows: First, use a box razor knife to strip 5/8" of insulation from the end of the cable. Be careful not to cut the copper strands inside.

Next, fill the lug half full with an anti-corrosion compound such as Noalox, or Cual-Aid. These compounds were developed when aluminum wiring was popular in homes, to prevent corrosion where the dissimilar metals met in copper/aluminum connections. It works very well for our application as well.

Carefully slide the bare copper into the lug, and wipe off any excess anti-corrosion compound that oozes out. Place the crimper on a hard, flat, stable surface. Put the lug in the crimper, with the flat side down and the thick part centered under the punch. Strike the top of the punch with a hammer until the punch doesn't move any more.

Tap upward with the hammer on the release stud on the back of the tool to free the lug. To test the crimp, lock the lug in a vise and tug sharply on the cable. You should be able to lean your weight against the cable and not loosen the crimp.

The final step is to slide a 1 1/2" piece of 1" diameter shrink tube over the lug and center it on the lug/cable joint. Shrink the tube into place with a heat gun.

If you don't have a heat gun, you can use a hand-held propane torch by holding the cable assembly about 3" from the visible end of the blue flame. You might want to practice this on some scrap shrink tube and cable first.

Don't try using a hair drier——it will take forever.

I have cut open lugs crimped this way many years later, and found no corrosion inside at all. I have never had a failure from this type of crimp.

"If necessary, a lug can be bent at an angle for a better fit."

When you are making short cables to connect components, you will want to make sure the lugs are oriented correctly for the connections they need to make. To do this, crimp one lug on first, and install it loosely in its proper position. Then run the cable to the other connection, and mark the cable end and the lug with a crayon to indicate how they should line up.

If necessary, a lug can be bent at an angle for a better fit. This is easy to do in a bench vise. Figure out the angle you need, bend it carefully, then leave it alone. Too much bending back and forth to find the right fit will fatigue and weaken the lug.

In general, the assembly sequence for mounting a cable to a terminal of any component should be: component terminal, cable lug, flat washer, lock washer, nut. The flat washer is there to keep the lock washer from gouging the cable lug. On the controller, you have flat terminals instead of threaded stud terminals. In that case you start with the bolt, and follow the same sequence, ending with a nylock nut.

The following wiring instructions assume that you are using an Albright main contactor, a Curtis/PMC controller, and a series brush DC motor, since these are by far the most commonly-used choices.

Starting at what will be the most positive cable out of the battery pack, the circuit breaker is the next component in the circuit (unless it's located between two batteries in the pack). Connect the cable to the breaker terminals using lugs with 3/8" holes, as opposed to the 5/16" hole lugs you will use for the batteries. The circuit breaker terminals are not polarized. Mount the breaker however is most convenient.

The next component is the main contactor. The cable from the battery pack and/or circuit breaker will mount to the large diameter positive terminal of the contactor, using a 3/8" lug.

The next connection is between the unmarked terminal of the main contactor and the battery positive terminal of the controller (again using a 3/8" lug for the contactor connection, but a 5/16" lug for the controller connection). If the contactor and controller are mounted very close together, it is almost impossible to get a tiny length of cable in there, but a short piece of copper strap will work nicely. It should be insulated except at the connections, using shrink tube. In the Voltsrabbit™, this requires a specific twist in the strap, using a bench vise and a large crescent wrench.

Any time you are making connections to controller terminals, use two wrenches, and be careful not to put any force on the terminal itself. It is possible to crack the potting around the base of the terminal, which could let moisture seep inside and short out the circuits.

There are two options for the next connection. One option is from the battery positive controller terminal to the A1 terminal of the motor. The second option skips the controller, and connects directly from the unmarked terminal of the contactor to the A1 motor terminal. The motor can be connected either way, depending on which is more convenient. The contactor and motor both use 3/8" lugs, while the controller uses 5/16" lugs.

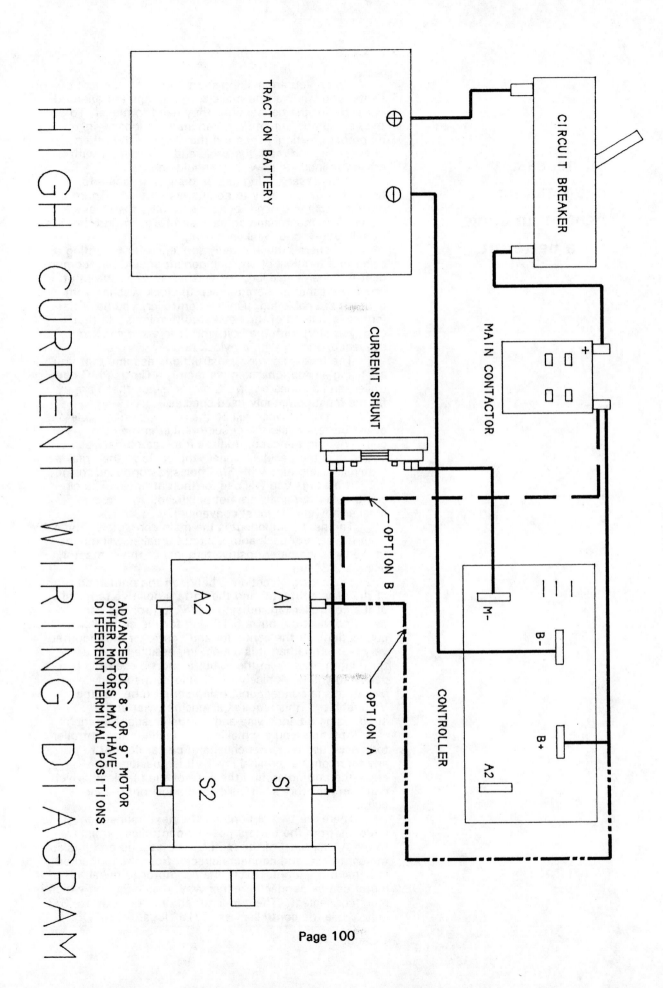

HIGH CURRENT WIRING DIAGRAM

TRACTION BATTERY

CIRCUIT BREAKER

MAIN CONTACTOR

CURRENT SHUNT

OPTION B

OPTION A

CONTROLLER

M-

B-

B+

A2

A1

A2

S1

S2

ADVANCED DC 8" OR 9" MOTOR
OTHER MOTORS MAY HAVE
DIFFERENT TERMINAL POSITIONS.

Use two wrenches when fastening lugs to controller terminals.

The next connection is on the motor itself. On a series motor running counterclockwise, the A2 motor terminal needs to be connected to the S2 terminal. Check the markings on your motor to identify which terminals these are. On some motors they will be side by side, and on others they will be diagonal to each other. The motor terminals all use 3/8" lugs. When these terminals are in a straight line, it is easy to connect them with a copper strap. Insulate all but the connecting ends of the strap with shrink tube.

The final cable from the motor attaches to the S1 terminal, and goes from there to the shunt.

On a car such as a Honda, where the motor needs to rotate clockwise, the wiring will be reversed. The input to the motor will be the A2 terminal, and the A1 will connect to the S2. The S1 terminal will be the outgoing cable.

I put the shunt here in the circuit because I prefer to have the ammeter read motor current. I find this to be the most useful information. The other choice would be to put the shunt between the battery negative controller terminal and the battery pack most negative cable. This gives the battery pack current reading. If you were to do this, the cable from the motor would go directly to the motor negative terminal of the controller.

If you really like lots of data, you can always put shunts in both places and have two gauges, or one gauge with a toggle switch.

The outgoing cable from the motor will connect to one of the large shunt terminals using a 3/8" lug. It doesn't matter which terminal.

From the shunt (or from the motor if the shunt is elsewhere), the cable connects to the motor negative terminal of the controller with a 5/16" lug.

The final cable is from the battery negative terminal of the controller to the most negative cable from the battery pack, using 5/16" lugs on both ends.

You will notice that the controller A2 terminal is

not used. This terminal is for an original equipment manufacturer (OEM) industrial vehicle application that does not apply to passenger car conversions.

Installing Batteries

When all the other wiring has been completed, it's time to install the battery racks and boxes permanently, install the batteries, and wire them up.

Install the batteries according to the layout drawings you made earlier, paying special attention to the proper orientation of the positive and negative posts.

Before connecting the batteries, be sure the circuit breaker and ignition key are both turned off. Batteries can be connected with short lengths of 2/0 cable, or with copper straps. I prefer the copper straps. These should be 1" wide and 1/16" thick, and all but the contact ends should be insulated with 3/4" shrink tube.

The straps should have at least one bend in them, to give them some springiness when the batteries move a little under normal road jostling. A completely rigid interconnect could put pressure on the battery posts and damage them.

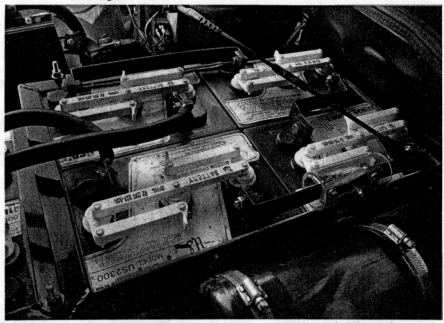

A battery pack using copper strap interconnects. Note fusible link in one interconnect.

Drill 5/16" holes in the strap ends and deburr them before bending the straps. Also, slide the shrink tube onto the strap before bending it, then shrink it into place afterwards.

You will probably have one or two interconnect shapes, such as ']', which will fit most of your connections. Bends are usually simple 90° bends, and can be done easily with a bench vise.

Each battery pack should have a fusible link in its circuit. This is easy to install in the middle of a long straight interconnect. Simply cut a section out of the middle of the interconnect, and attach the two cut ends of the cable or strap to the ends of the fusible link, making it a part of the interconnect. I like to mount the link on a plexiglass block to give it a little extra rigidity, and slide it into a clear plex tube to contain it if it should blow.

I recommend applying some type of anti-corrosion compound to the battery posts and interconnect ends before connecting them. This can be Noalox or Cual-Aid, or a spray liquid called Corrosion Block. I recommend applying either type with a small brush. If you are using the spray liquid, spray some of it into a small container and brush it on from there.

Noalox and Cual-Aid come as a grey paste. They can remain a little sticky to the touch, but they do a good job. The Corrosion Block is a thin purple liquid which dries completely. Its one drawback is that it attracts and kills small insects, so you will have to clear dead flies and gnats from your battery posts occasionally.

There are numerous other brands and similar products available at electrical and electronic suppliers. Each will have slightly different advantages and disadvantages. For example, for years I used a product called Korode Kure. It was a black tarry substance which you painted all over the post after the cable was attached. It did a great job, but would get runny with heat and drip down the side of the battery, looking really ugly.

Once the battery post and interconnect are treated with the chemical of your choice, they need to be bolted together. Insert a 5/16" bolt through a flat washer, then through the battery post, then through the interconnect. On the other end of the bolt, install a Belleville washer with the concave side facing the interconnect, and a nut. Tighten using two insulated battery wrenches.

The Belleville washer is a special washer to prevent the connection from loosening due to 'cold creep' of the lead in the battery post. The washer is concave in shape, with a much more precise and uniform spring tension than ordinary lock washers. In some industrial applications it is actually used as a calibrated spring. It will keep a constant pressure against the connection without gouging the interconnect.

Install all the battery connections except the ones containing the fusible links, and the ones leading into and out of each battery pack. These will be connected one by one in the 'smoke test'.

Test Points

If the most positive and most negative terminals of your entire battery pack are difficult to reach with a voltmeter, you might want to wire in a convenient test point for total pack voltage.

I do this with two one-foot lengths of 16 gauge wire, red and black, tie-wrapped into a loom. One goes to the large diameter positive main contactor terminal. the other goes to the battery negative controller terminal. The free ends can be crimped into insulated female connectors, which will accept a meter probe. An insulated connector has an insulating sheath covering the entire connector, not just the barrel.

This will give you a quick easy place to plug in and test full pack voltage.

Page 103

11

Final Hookup & Bench Testing

"I imagine myself as an electron traveling through the circuit."

Now comes the part that takes nerve——the 'smoke test'. It's time to make the final connections and see if you did it right. By the way, these are the same tests to use for troubleshooting later if you should have a failure in the electrical system and you need a systematic way to track it down.

We'll do this in a careful progression, working from one end of the car to the other, testing each section in isolation before joining it to the previously tested sections and then retesting. The key to troubleshooting electrical systems is to test each possible failure point separately, so you can identify the exact source of the problem, and to do it systematically, so you don't miss any possibilities. I imagine myself as an electron traveling through the circuit, and I test each point along the way where there might be a problem.

For each test, I will tell you several things to check if you don't get the right results. Then we'll assume you've found and corrected any problems, and we'll move on to the next test.

If you were careful when you did the wiring, you probably won't need to use any of these checks to trace problems, so I'll make it easy for you to skip over them. I'll indent the troubleshooting sections so that, if you don't need them, you can skip ahead to the next hook-up stage.

I'm assuming you have a car with the batteries split between front and rear packs, because this is the most common configuration. If your car has more or fewer packs, it should be easy to tell which steps to repeat or skip.

I'm also assuming that your circuit breaker is in the middle of the positive cable from the batteries to the main contactor. If your circuit breaker is actually in the middle of a battery pack, you will need to close it and test it when you test that pack.

We'll start testing at the pack that connects to the main contactor positive terminal. For purposes of discussion, we'll call this the most positive pack.

Be sure that: the circuit breaker is off, the onboard charger is disconnected from the batteries at the Anderson connector, the negative cable from the next pack is not touching any battery terminal or chassis, the ignition key is off, the negative cable of the auxiliary battery is disconnected and not touching anything, the parking brake is on, and the car is out of gear. Raise the drive end of the car and support it with jackstands. For front wheel drive cars, position the jack under the point where the transmission and adaptor mate to lift.

Locate the final battery interconnect in the most positive pack. This won't necessarily be the last one in the circuit, physically. It will be the one containing the fusible link, the only one you haven't installed yet. Touch it lightly across the battery terminals where it will be installed. If there is no spark, install the interconnect.

If there is a spark, remove the interconnect and recheck the battery orientations and interconnects against your original diagram. If those are correct, check for shorts in the positive cable going out of the pack. Recheck that the negative cable is not touching anything.

With a voltmeter, check the most positive and most negative terminals of this battery pack. The reading between them should be about 48 volts for an eight battery pack. For other sizes of packs, it should be the voltage of each battery (usually 6 volts) multiplied by the number of batteries.

If the voltage reading isn't correct, check all the interconnects, and check each individual battery for full voltage.

Checking battery pack voltage with a voltmeter.

Turn on the circuit breaker. Use the voltmeter to check the voltage between the circuit breaker/battery pack positive terminal of the main contactor and the negative cable out of the most positive pack. The voltage should be the same as in the previous test.

If the voltage reading isn't right, check for an open circuit between the main contactor and the most positive terminal of the battery pack.

Turn the circuit breaker off again, and move to the next battery pack in the circuit. Do not connect the cable between this pack and the previous one yet.

Install the final interconnect containing the fusible link for this pack, using the same touch-test as before.

Use the voltmeter to measure between the most positive and most negative battery terminals of this pack. The reading should match the voltage total for this pack.

If the voltage reading isn't right, check battery orientations and interconnects against your diagram.

Install the negative cable from the second pack to the first (most positive) pack. Use the same touch-test technique you used when installing the fusible links.

Turn the circuit breaker on again. Measure the voltage between the most negative terminal of the second pack and the circuit breaker/battery pack positive terminal of the main contactor. The reading should be the sum of the two packs.

If you have more than two packs, continue down the circuit this way until you have checked and connected them all.

When all the packs are connected in series, check for full pack voltage between the battery pack/positive terminal of the main contactor and the battery negative terminal of the controller. This can be done at the test point (if you wired one in).

If the meter does not read full pack voltage, recheck all previous connections.

Checking for full pack voltage at a test point.

Connect the voltmeter between the controller terminal of the main contactor (the negative terminal) and the most negative terminal of the most negative battery pack. The reading should be 0 volts.

Connect the chassis ground cable or strap to the auxiliary battery negative terminal.

Turn on the ignition key. Nothing should happen.

If you hear a click from the main contactor and the voltmeter reading goes from zero to full pack voltage, do the following checks.

Recheck that the potbox arm rests at full 'off', which opens the potbox microswitch. If the lever arm is at full 'off' and the microswitch is open as it should be, turn off the ignition and check for continuity between the first and third small terminals of the potbox. If there is continuity, replace the microswitch.

With the ignition on, actuate the potbox lever by hand. Now you should hear a click from the main contactor, and the reading on the voltmeter should go to full pack voltage. If this doesn't happen, do the following checks.

Check for 12 volts between the main contactor negative terminal (bottom small terminal opposite diode) and the auxiliary battery positive terminal. If you don't have 12 volts here, check the ground to the mounting screw of the potbox relay.

Check for 12 volts between the leftmost terminal on the potbox microswitch and any chassis ground. If you don't have 12 volts here, check the wiring loom installation between the ignition key and the potbox, and check the charger interlock wiring.

If both of those readings are correct but the main contactor still won't close, actuate the potbox lever arm and check for 12 volts from the rightmost potbox microswitch terminal. If you don't get 12 volts, replace the microswitch.

If all the previous measurements are correct but the main contactor still won't close, check for voltage between the main contactor positive terminal (top small terminal opposite diode) and the chassis ground with the potbox lever arm actuated. If the meter reads 12 volts, replace the main contactor. If the meter reads 0 volts, check the wire between the main contactor positive terminal and the rightmost terminal of the potbox microswitch for continuity. If you don't have continuity, fix the wire.

Once the main contactor closes as it should and you have full pack voltage, turn off the ignition. Connect the cable between the battery negative terminal of the controller and the negative terminal of the last battery in the most negative pack.

Be sure the car is in neutral. Turn the ignition on. Actuate the potbox either with the throttle pedal or by hand. The main contactor should close and the motor should start turning. If the motor does not start turning, do the following checks.

Check for full pack voltage at the key switch input terminal of the controller. Do this by connecting the voltmeter between the battery negative terminal of the controller and the key switch positive terminal (top 1/4" male terminal), and then actuating the potbox.

If the reading is not full pack voltage, check the wiring for continuity between the key switch input terminal and the potbox relay. If there is continuity, check for full pack voltage to the movable arm terminal of the potbox relay. If there is not full pack voltage to this terminal, check the wire between the relay terminal and the circuit breaker/battery pack positive terminal of the main contactor for continuity.

If all the previous checks are correct, check all other potbox relay wiring. If that is correct, check the potbox relay itself for mechanical failure by actuating the potbox with the ignition on, and listening or feeling for the relay to close. If the relay does not close, replace it.

If the reading at the key switch input terminal of the controller is full pack voltage but the motor does not turn, check the potbox. To do this, remove the black and white wires from the second and third 1/4" male terminals of the controller. Connect the ohm-meter positive probe to the black wire and the negative probe to the white wire. The reading should be between 1 and 1.4 ohms.

Now actuate the potbox lever arm. The reading should climb to 5 kohms at full open. If it doesn't, replace the potbox.

If the potbox operates correctly, connect the voltmeter positive probe to the battery positive terminal of the controller and the negative probe to the motor side of the shunt. Turn on the ignition and actuate the potbox. The reading should go to full pack voltage almost immediately. If there is no output, replace the controller.

If the controller operates correctly, check connections to the motor. If the connections are good, there is an internal problem in the motor.

Put the car into first gear. Actuate the potbox lever arm with the throttle pedal or by hand and observe which direction the wheels turn.

If the wheels turn backward, recheck the motor connections.

Turn off the car, put it into neutral, set the handbrake, and remove the jackstands.

Connect the charger at the Anderson connector, then test and adjust it according to its manufacturer's instructions.

Do not attempt to break a bottle of champagne over the bumper, or even pour it over the bumper. It's bad for the chrome and paint, and a waste of champagne.

Besides, you're not done yet.

"If the wheels turn backward, recheck the motor connections."

12

Suspension & Tires

Springs

When you remove the jackstands and lower the car, you will immediately notice a change in it. It is now a lowrider. This condition needs to be remedied before you do any serious driving.

Drive the car——carefully——just far enough to get it properly settled on its springs. If you don't have any serious interference problems, you might want to drive it to the public scale and get it weighed again: the whole car, and each end separately. Then remeasure the ride height at all four corners.

Compare these numbers to the pre-conversion numbers in your Project Notebook. You now know exactly how much weight it gained, and where, and how many inches of ride height it lost.

Or gained. If a car is heavy on one end and light on the other, the leverage effect will cause the light end to sit higher than before. Often adjusting the heavy end will automatically correct the light end, too. However, it is better for handling purposes if the weight is more evenly distributed in the first place.

The suspension may be coil springs, leaf springs, or torsion bars. Roughly the same options exist for all three types, with a couple of exceptions which I will point out.

The easiest option is to find a bolt-in set of heavier duty springs. To do this, check with your parts connection at the dealership to see if there is another model of car with heavier springs that would bolt in.

Aftermarket overload leaf springs on a Datsun pickup.

This may actually be another, heavier model of car, or it may be another version of your model with a larger engine, air conditioning, or a towing package. If you can identify some appropriate parts, then you can try to locate them in a wrecking yard.

If you have no luck with the dealer, try the aftermarket parts house. Some models of cars are more prone to owner 'modification' than others, and there are likely to be aftermarket overload springs available for those. Be sure to get good quality springs. It will mean paying more, but it's well worth it. Also, avoid the 'coil spring helpers'. These are little devices you install between the coils. They essentially prevent the spring from compressing fully, as it's intended to do.

The third option is having custom springs built. This option is not available for torsion bar suspensions. However, some torsion bars are adjustable, which is an option not offered by coil or leaf springs.

For custom springs, the spring company will want to know how much weight was added to each axle, how much ride height was lost, all the physical dimensions of the original springs both unloaded and fully loaded, the shape of the spring ends where they install in the car, and the spring rate. That final number may be in your shop manual, and it may not.

The easiest way to get custom springs is to provide the car weight and ride height information, and the old springs. The custom springs may *look* identical to the originals—same height, diameter, thickness, and number of coils. The secret is in the spring rate, or degree of stiffness, of the spring material.

There is one final suspension option for coil springs that do not enclose the shock absorber: air shocks. These are readily available, affordable, easy to install, adjustable, and reliable if the plumbing is properly done. I have had them in several vehicles for many years with no failures.

If you have trouble finding an air shock to fit your car, there are ways to track them down. Get your aftermarket parts man to let you look through his KYB shock catalog. This is a wonderful reference. It has charts showing which model of KYB shocks fit which cars—and they have a model for almost anything. It also has full descriptions and pictures of each type of shock, giving all the dimensions and showing the mounting style of the ends.

Match the description and drawing to the original shocks for your car, and note the designation for that particular KYB shock. Now go back through the application charts and see what other cars use the same KYB shock your car uses. Then ask your parts man if there is an air shock kit for one of those other models. Pickup trucks are especially good bets. You may find, as I did, that there are no air shock kits for a Plymouth Arrow, but plenty of them for a 4x4 Nissan truck, which uses the same shock.

Shocks

While we're on the subject, let's talk about shocks a little more. The term 'shock absorber' is a misnomer. A shock is really an oscillation dampener. The springs support the weight of the car, and compress and expand to diminish the effect of bumps. The shocks provide resistance to gently stop the springs from compressing and expanding (i.e., bouncing) once the bump is past.

"Air shocks are readily available, affordable, easy to install, adjustable, and reliable."

In an EV, there's a lot more weight moving up and down on those springs, so it's a good idea to have heavier duty shocks to help dampen that extra weight in motion.

I like the KYB brand, personally, especially the Gas-A-Just model. I have no stock in the company; I have just used the product for many years and have been very satisfied with it. They cover a broad range of models. There are several other very fine brands of heavy duty shocks.

One word of warning on McPherson struts: DO NOT attempt to replace a strut cartridge in the safety and comfort of your own garage. The struts are compressed— under a great deal of pressure—and held in place by one bolt. If you loosen that bolt without having the spring properly restrained, the strut will turn into an unguided missile.

Instead, I recommend removing the entire strut assembly from the car and taking it to a shop that specializes in that make of car. They will have a professional spring compressor specifically for that purpose. The one I have mounts to the wall, has a safety cage to contain the spring, and uses air shocks to compress the spring.

Don't buy or rent one of the cheap 'spring compressor tools' that are available. They will only get you hurt. These consist of a couple of pieces of readybolt with hooks on them. The theory is that you crank the hooks down on the readybolt, and the hooks compress the spring. In real life, as you crank down, the hooks simply start to walk around the spring.

Tires

The kind of tires you have on your EV will make a big difference in its handling and range. The first rule is: radials only, no bias ply tires. Almost everybody uses radials these days anyway, but it bears emphasizing. Bias tires simply cannot stand the stresses an EV will put on them.

The most important feature in tires for an EV is low rolling resistance. Rolling resistance includes the friction of the tire against the pavement, which is necessary for traction and handling, but it also includes frictions inside the tire as it changes shape while rolling and the cords move against each other.

At this time, the best tires available are the Goodyear Invicta GL and GLFE models. They are not yet available in all sizes, but it would be worth changing wheels to fit them on your car. These tires were developed as a result of research by Goodyear on tires for the GM Impact. The key is a completely new design for the internal tire structure that lowers rolling resistance without losing traction or handling. At highway cruise speeds, they will save you up to 50 amps.

I have two Voltsrabbits^{TM}, which are identical except that one has Invictas, and the other has ordinary steel radials. The difference in performance is impressive. I have a friend with a very light three-wheeled EV with Invictas. If he parks it on the flat without using a parking brake, a slight breeze will roll the car.

The word today in low rolling resistance tires is Goodyear Invicta.

There will probably be continuous improvements in low rolling resistance tires, so I recommend checking on the latest developments.

Air pressure is also critical to rolling resistance. It's very important in an EV to keep the tires properly inflated. On the Goodyears, this means at the rated maximum pressure.

If you are interested in experimenting, it's easy to check this out for yourself. One method is to find a deserted piece of road with a gentle hill. Allow the car to roll down the hill, propelled entirely by gravity, and see where it finally stops. Next, alter the tire pressure and try it again. Another method is to drive a specific stretch of road at a constant speed in a specific gear, and check your amp draw. Then change the tire pressure and do it again. The results are very clear.

Alignment

After the suspension and tires are set up the way they will stay, take the car to a good alignment shop and get both ends aligned. Poor alignment will wear your tires prematurely, and seriously compromise the car's performance.

NOW, you're ready for the real road test.

13

Road Test, Driving, & Paperwork

Road Test

Don't plan to road test the conversion by driving it to work Monday morning. For the first drive, around the block is plenty. Don't drive in heavy traffic, and don't drive further than you would be willing to walk home. Be sure you have your safety kit with you.

The car will feel a little strange to you. You may be surprised how much you used auditory cues in a gas car without being aware of it. Pay attention to the feel of the throttle, clutch and brakes, and if they feel different, play with them a little until you start to feel comfortable with them. Notice how the car feels in corners or on hills.

After you've driven around the block a few times, stop the car and get out and inspect it. Look for anything that might have shaken loose or started to rub, sniff for any alarming smells. Put your hand (carefully!) on the controller, motor, and battery terminals and see how warm they are. Anything that is hot after a short easy drive indicates a problem that needs to be corrected.

In some ways, an EV is like a pet. It will be easier for you to recognize an 'illness' if you know what 'normal' looks, sounds, smells, and feels like. You should spend the first month paying extra attention to all these things so you really get to know your car and its behavior.

Before you put your EV into daily service, examine some of your normal commuting and errand routes from your gas car. Note mileage, average traffic speeds, hills, amount of stops or freeway. If part of your route includes a long hill, or lots of stop-and-go traffic, look for a different route that may climb the same hill in stages, or move traffic more smoothly.

You may want to spend an afternoon testing your car for range. (Remember, this range will improve as both car and driver get broken in.) To test range, lay out a flat route with little traffic and few stops. Plan a loop of no more than a couple of miles. With the batteries fully charged, drive the course at a steady speed between 25 - 45 mph, which is the range where most daily driving is done. At each lap, note the mileage, state-of-charge or voltage at rest, and amp draw at cruise. You may want to stop every few laps and feel the motor, controller, and battery terminals for temperature, just to familiarize yourself with their normal patterns.

You will notice, as your pack voltage falls off, your amp draw will increase. Unlike a gas car, which runs at full performance until it runs out of gas and stops dead, an EV will gradually lose power over a span of several miles as it draws to the bottom of its charge. Eventually, it can keep crawling along at a walking pace for a surprising distance. This can be handy if you have to limp home, but not something you want to do as a matter of course. Crawling along at less than 5 mph is

"In some ways, an EV is like a pet."

Page 113

not recommended, especially uphill, as high amp draws at low speeds can damage the controller.

You will have to choose a point that you consider 'out of juice', a point on the state-of-charge or voltmeter at which the car is too underpowered for you to feel comfortable in traffic. Once you know what that feels like and looks like on your gauges, on a safe street close to home with no traffic, you will feel more confident in traffic and away from home. Test the car's limits.

In the course of these practice drives, you will discover another way in which an 'out-of-fuel' EV differs from a gas car. An EV has a built-in emergency reserve tank. In fact, it has several. When the car is 'out-of-juice', you can pull over to the shoulder and rest it for ten minutes or so, and watch the voltmeter climb as the batteries 'grow charge'. Simply resting will allow the batteries to naturally recover a certain amount of their charge, which is enough to allow you to drive a few more miles. This resting recharge can be done several times if necessary, although it is not recommended as a regular procedure.

There is always a certain smug satisfaction in driving to the grocery store, arriving with 90% of charge remaining, doing the shopping, and returning to a car that says it has 100% of charge. Try that with a gas car!

Now you will feel ready to fly a little farther from the nest. On a Sunday, drive your usual route to work, and learn how the car feels on those streets without the stress of needing to punch in at a certain time.

Now you're ready to put the car into real daily service. There are a few things you need to know to understand what your car is doing and get the best performance from it.

Breaking In

As I mentioned earlier, there is a breaking-in period. This applies to three things: the batteries, the motor, and the driver. Performance will gradually increase until all three are fully broken in.

New batteries are 'green', and will achieve only 90 - 95% of full capacity until they have been through 20 - 50 charge/discharge cycles. These may be partial or full discharges.

Motor brushes require about 20 hours of operation to seat properly before the motor will operate at full efficiency. As the brushes wear in, the motor will become quieter and quieter.

Driving an EV for optimum performance requires many of the same techniques as driving a gas car for optimum fuel efficiency. These include smooth acceleration and deceleration, and watching traffic flow ahead to maintain as even a pace as possible, minimizing the need for braking or sudden changes in speed or direction.

However, optimum EV driving also requires some different techniques from those used on combustion engine cars. There will be a learning period before the driver operates at full efficiency.

"There is a breaking-in period for three things: the batteries, the motor, and the driver."

Driving

Use the clutch to accelerate out of a stop. Revving the motor up *a little* before slipping the clutch will give you smooth yet sprightly acceleration. Not using the clutch gives a jolting but more sluggish start. It is not necessary—nor recommended—to apply more than a little throttle with the clutch in, and then only briefly. *Operating the motor at high rpm, especially with no load on it, could damage the motor.*

On acceleration, the ammeter will peg at 400 amps, then begin to fall off. It will stabilize around 150 - 200 amps. At the same time, the voltmeter or state-of-charge meter will fall off sharply, then climb gradually and stabilize. This means you have reached the maximum potential for that gear. To continue accelerating, shift up.

When shifting gears, shift quickly while holding the throttle half open. The *momentary* rev between gears will help keep motor rpm high for best power and efficiency. *Operating the motor in neutral other than briefly between gears is not recommended, and could damage the motor.*

At this time, there are no commercially available regenerative braking systems for the home mechanic to install. For that reason, the majority of EVs for some time to come will probably not have regenerative braking. Without engine braking, the car will not slow down for quite a while when you remove your foot from the throttle on a flat road. You will discover there are many times when little or no throttle is needed to maintain speed.

On hills, expect to shift down sooner than necessary in a gas car. With practice, the 'feel' of the car and the ammeter will teach you when to be in third, second, or even first gear. Climbing hills in too high a gear can damage your motor or controller. When in doubt, shift down.

If you are climbing a hill and increased throttle does not increase your speed, back off the throttle until you reach the point where the car responds to it again. That is the best performance you will get in that gear, and any additional throttle will only waste amps and heat up the motor and controller. The motor has sufficient torque to pull hills comfortably at low speeds. If the car feels like it's losing power, shift down and find the optimum throttle position for that gear.

More throttle does not always equal more speed. In simplistic terms, amps equal torque and volts equal speed. More throttle gives more amps, which decreases pack voltage. If half throttle has adequate torque for the job, more throttle will waste amperage *and* reduce voltage, i.e., speed. In other words, sometimes you can climb a grade as fast *or faster* at half throttle than at full throttle, and use less energy.

After cresting a hill and starting down, BE SURE TO SHIFT UP. *If you coast at too high a speed in a low gear, you may over-rev and damage the motor. For the same reason, be sure the car is in neutral if it is being towed.*

When the throttle is released for coasting, the ammeter will drop to 0 because no power is being consumed. There is also no engine braking, so it will be necessary to use the brakes more, as with an automatic

"After cresting a hill and starting down, BE SURE TO SHIFT UP."

transmission. It is better to apply the brakes periodically to slow down, then release them to coast up to speed, then brake again, rather than riding them continuously down a hill, which may cause the brakes to overheat and lose performance.

You will be surprised to find that downhill momentum will carry you farther up the next hill than it would in a gas car. With practice, you can learn to use this to great advantage, and sometimes travel several miles using very little throttle or none at all.

It is not necessary to use the clutch to brake to a stop. If you do use the clutch, leave it in (or put the car in neutral) for several moments after the car stops. The momentum of the flywheel will keep the motor spinning for some time. If you coast to a complete stop with the clutch in, then release it before the motor stops spinning, the car will buck.

Use extra care in parking lots and around pedestrians, bicyclists, and animals. The car is virtually silent, and may not be noticed as it approaches.

Performance of the car does not decrease steadily with battery pack discharge, nor does it stop abruptly, as it does when a gas car is out of fuel. Instead, performance remains fairly consistent throughout most of the car's range. As the pack nears total depletion, the car will grow gradually more sluggish over the last five to ten miles.

Gauges & Warnings

The ammeter is your 'efficiency gauge'. By varying gears and throttle pressure while watching for the lowest current reading, you can determine the most efficient technique for accelerating, maintaining speed, or climbing a hill. Since an electric car is typically used on the same routes repeatedly, you can develop the optimum technique for each portion of your normal drive. Typical readings will be:

400 amps for momentary full acceleration
100 amps cruising on flat roads
200 amps on slight grades
300 amps on steep grades
0 when coasting

Lower amp draws also mean cooler operating temperatures—and less stress—for the motor and controller.

In simplistic terms, amperage increases as voltage decreases. You can verify this by watching your gauges as you accelerate. This is one reason a 96-volt system is better than a 72-volt system. With higher voltage available, it needs less amperage. This is also the reason why an EV is most efficient at high rpm, meaning the top safe speed (below 'redline') for a particular gear. In general, higher rpm means higher voltage and speed but lower amperage and torque.

Your car may have a voltmeter for battery pack voltage, or a state-of-charge meter. We talked earlier about the specific peculiarities of sampling-type state-of-charge meters. We'll talk here about how to use a real-time analog state-of-charge meter or voltmeter.

Both of these gauges provide the same information. The state-of-charge displays it as a percentage from 0 to

"The ammeter is your 'efficiency gauge'."

100%, which is what we are all used to in gas cars. The voltmeter will give you more precise information measured in actual voltage, but it will require some interpretation from you to determine state-of-charge.

These gauges will fluctuate with the throttle: as you depress the throttle, the ammeter will climb and the state-of-charge meter or voltmeter will drop while you 'draw down' the voltage in the pack. For an accurate state-of-charge reading, check the gauge when you are completely off the throttle, either coasting or at a stop.

A battery that is 20% discharged is considered 'empty'. The state-of-charge meter is calibrated to read 0% at that 'empty' voltage, which is approximately 83 volts on a 96-volt system.

This can be a little confusing. A 6-volt battery, when fully charged, is actually at about 6.5 volts. That means that a fully charged 96-volt pack is actually at about 104 volts. If you are using a voltmeter, the scale should extend about 10% higher than the nominal voltage of your pack. Eighty percent of the actual fully charged voltage is your official 'empty' point.

If this sounds complicated, that's why most people prefer a simple state-of-charge gauge.

In the wiring section, we talked about wiring one of the original dash warning lights, such as the alternator light, to be a 'key-on' indicator. This will come on any time the key is turned on, and does not indicate any problem.

The other rewired original dash indicator, possibly an oil pressure light, is now a motor temperature light. If that comes on, STOP IMMEDIATELY and allow the motor to cool while determining the cause of the overheating. A motor can overheat from driving too slow in a high gear, or pulling a grade for an extended time. Amps equal heat. High amperage for too long will cause overheating. General rule of thumb: do not exceed 250 amps for more than 5 minutes continuously.

Like any motor or engine, an EV motor will self-destruct if it is forced to turn faster than it was intended to turn. For this reason, it is important not to tow the car in gear, or drive or coast faster than the top rated speed for each gear.

On a Rabbit with stock wheels and tires, these speed worked out to be 25 mph in first gear, 45 mph in second, and 67 mph in third. Interestingly enough, these were almost identical to the original factory recommended shift points, as marked on the speedometer.

To calculate these top speeds for each gear for your car, use the following formula:

$$MPH = \frac{RPM \times R}{G_1 \times G_2 \times 168}$$

MPH = maximum speed for the gear specified by G_1
RPM = rated motor rpm at pack voltage
R = rolling radius of drive wheel tires in inches
G_1 = gear ratio for specific gear
G_2 = final drive ratio
168 = constant value

"Like any motor or engine, an electric motor will self-destruct if it is forced to turn faster than it was intended to turn."

For example, for a VW Bug using an Advanced D.C. 8"
motor and a 96-volt system, the formula for top speed for
first gear would be:

$$MPH = \frac{5,000 \times 12}{3.8 \times 4.375 \times 168}$$

$$MPH = \frac{60,000}{2,793}$$

$$MPH = 21.48$$

If the controller becomes too hot, it will reduce
power and emit a high whistle. Pull off the road to
allow the controller to cool down, and determine why it
is overheating. These controllers have functioned in
race conditions in $100^o + F$ temperatures, so this should
not occur in normal driving, except possibly on a long
steep grade.

If the voltage to the controller drops too low, it
will reduce power to protect its circuits. This is most
likely to occur if the battery pack is very low and amp
demand is high. If this occurs, release the throttle
completely, then depress it again more gently. By de-
manding less amperage, you allow more voltage to pass
through. The motor has excellent low speed torque, and
can probably climb the hill adequately at a slightly
slower speed.

The controller includes a high-pedal lockout safety
feature which will not allow the car to start with the
throttle depressed. If the car will not start, be sure
the throttle pedal is fully released and the potbox lever
arm is in the full 'off' position.

If you smell battery gasses while driving, it means
the batteries are discharging too hard and overheating.
If there is no heavy load on the car, such as a steep
hill, you need to check for low tires, dragging brakes,
or a failing battery.

Stop immediately at any smell of burning insulation
and turn off both the ignition and circuit breaker.
Check all the high current connections visually, and
check for heat carefully by holding your hands near the
connections. Don't continue driving until you identify
the source of the smell and correct it.

**"I recommend
keeping
a small log book
in the glovebox."**

Log Book
There is one more book to add to your conversion
library now: a log book. I recommend keeping a small
book in the glovebox and recording the daily routine and
noteworthy occurrences involving the car.

For example, I record the date, beginning mileage,
state of charge, itinerary, and ending mileage and state
of charge for each trip I take. I also note if there was
anything unusual about the trip, or when I added battery
water, and similar things.

This serves as a touchstone for 'normal'. I drive
the same routes, week after week. If I suddenly notice
that the state of charge is much lower than usual after a
grocery run, I know to start looking for a soggy tire or

other problem. The book is an excellent service record and diagnostic tool.

It's also a fun way to compete against yourself to improve your driving efficiency.

Paperwork

There are at least three kinds of paperwork related to EVs. The comments I will make here are necessarily general, because the regulations change from state to state, and from day to day, and I am simply trying to give you an overview. You will need to research the specific rules that apply currently in your location.

Registration. In most places, there is no problem registering an electric conversion. Outside of commercial applications, there are generally no special registration requirements. Most states are interested in encouraging alternative fueled vehicles, and may actually offer incentives.

In California, you will need to take your conversion to the Department of Motor Vehicles. Have them verify that it is a pure electric car and enter 'electric' as the fuel type on the title on the state computer. Then you will be exempted from smog tests.

Before buying your donor car, check your state's rules. Reviving a car that has been 'scrapped' officially, or is not driveable, can involve extra hassle to get a clear title. A car with a lapsed registration may have hefty penalties attached to it.

Insurance. The insurance companies are still developing their policies and procedures for electric conversions. Full coverage will be harder to get than liability.

Work with an agent you already have a good relationship with, if possible. Otherwise, try to find an agent who has already insured conversions.

This is one place where the sedate image of the electric may pay off. Emphasize that this is a local-use car. You may actually get a lower rate.

Incentives. There are numerous incentives springing up for electric cars, at levels from city to federal. You may be able to campaign for more incentives in your area.

Some of these incentives include sales tax exemptions, and income tax credits. The local utility may offer cash incentives, or a special meter for overnight charging at a lower rate. You may acquire smog credits that you can sell. Employers who are under pressure to clean up the employee fleet may be happy to install a charging station for you. There may be preferential parking areas, or exemptions for using carpool freeway lanes.

If there is an air quality management district in your area, or a state energy or environmental office, they may be able to help you find some of these incentives.

If you find a lack of incentives in your area, or rules that are actively unfriendly to electric conversions, contact your elected officials (from the city level to the federal level) and ask them why.

14

Charging & Maintenance

Charging

As in the rest of this book, we are talking about the most commonly used technology. In this instance, that means flooded lead-acid batteries. Be aware that some of the items mentioned here would not apply to other, more exotic battery types.

Before starting the car, the battery pack will have a 'surface charge' above its actual useable charge. For this reason, a 'full' car may show as high as 110% on the state-of-charge gauge. This surface charge will vanish as soon as you begin to drive.

This type of battery does not like to be left sitting in a discharged state. For this reason, you are encouraged to 'opportunity charge' whenever possible at your destination, or between short trips. It is especially important to recharge as soon as possible when the pack is deeply discharged and close to empty.

Always leave the battery caps on when charging.

The car will operate most efficiently, with best battery life and performance, if it is used often. If it sits for a week unused, it should be charged briefly to top up the batteries.

Some chargers have an automatic shut-off. Others simply taper to a low finish charge. If yours does not turn off automatically, it should be turned off soon after the car is fully charged.

The charger may have adjustable current. This is handy when you are charging away from home. If the circuit you plug into is rated lower than your usual charging outlet, you can reduce the current draw until the charger no longer throws the building's circuit breaker. You will charge more slowly, but you'll still be charging.

If you come out after a full charging period and find that all of the battery tops except one are damp, that one battery is failing. It is not accepting a full charge, and the charger is boiling the other batteries while trying to bring that one up.

If one or two batteries fail during the first two years or so, you can simply replace them. However, after the three year point, you should seriously consider replacing the whole pack. At that stage, if one or two are failing, others are probably not far behind. It is not good to mix new fresh batteries with old tired ones. The charger will be overcharging the new batteries (and shortening their lives) while trying to bring the old batteries up to match.

If you suspect you have a bad battery, do a voltage and specific gravity test on the whole pack. The following two pages are charts you can photocopy and use for 6-volt or 12-volt packs up to 144 volts.

This test should be done when the pack is fully charged, and has rested off the charger for a few hours. With a voltmeter, check the voltage on each battery. A fully charged 6-volt battery should read about 6.3 volts, and a fully charged 12-volt battery should read about 12.7 volts.

"The car will operate most efficiently, and have better battery life and performance, if it is used often."

BATTERY HYDROMETER TEST CHART—6 VOLT BATTERIES

DATE:_____   CAR:_____   PACK VOLTAGE:_____

BATTERY	CELL #1	CELL #2	CELL #3	BATTERY	CELL #1	CELL #2	CELL #3
#1 ___V				#13 ___V			
SP. GR.	_____	_____	_____	SP. GR.	_____	_____	_____
#2 ___V				#14 ___V			
SP. GR.	_____	_____	_____	SP. GR.	_____	_____	_____
#3 ___V				#15 ___V			
SP. GR.	_____	_____	_____	SP. GR.	_____	_____	_____
#4 ___V				#16 ___V			
SP. GR.	_____	_____	_____	SP. GR.	_____	_____	_____
#5 ___V				#17 ___V			
SP. GR.	_____	_____	_____	SP. GR.	_____	_____	_____
#6 ___V				#18 ___V			
SP. GR.	_____	_____	_____	SP. GR.	_____	_____	_____
#7 ___V				#19 ___V			
SP. GR.	_____	_____	_____	SP. GR.	_____	_____	_____
#8 ___V				#20 ___V			
SP. GR.	_____	_____	_____	SP. GR.	_____	_____	_____
#9 ___V				#21 ___V			
SP. GR.	_____	_____	_____	SP. GR.	_____	_____	_____
#10 ___V				#22 ___V			
SP. GR.	_____	_____	_____	SP. GR.	_____	_____	_____
#11 ___V				#23 ___V			
SP. GR.	_____	_____	_____	SP. GR.	_____	_____	_____
#12 ___V				#24 ___V			
SP. GR.	_____	_____	_____	SP. GR.	_____	_____	_____

BATTERY HYDROMETER TEST CHART—12 VOLT BATTERIES

DATE:_____   CAR:_____   PACK VOLTAGE:_____

BATTERY	CELL #1	CELL #2	CELL #3	CELL #4	CELL #5	CELL #6
#1 ____V						
SP. GR.	_____	_____	_____	_____	_____	_____
#2 ____V						
SP. GR.	_____	_____	_____	_____	_____	_____
#3 ____V						
SP. GR.	_____	_____	_____	_____	_____	_____
#4 ____V						
SP. GR.	_____	_____	_____	_____	_____	_____
#5 ____V						
SP. GR.	_____	_____	_____	_____	_____	_____
#6 ____V						
SP. GR.	_____	_____	_____	_____	_____	_____
#7 ____V						
SP. GR.	_____	_____	_____	_____	_____	_____
#8 ____V						
SP. GR.	_____	_____	_____	_____	_____	_____
#9 ____V						
SP. GR.	_____	_____	_____	_____	_____	_____
#10 ____V						
SP. GR.	_____	_____	_____	_____	_____	_____
#11 ____V						
SP. GR.	_____	_____	_____	_____	_____	_____
#12 ____V						
SP. GR.	_____	_____	_____	_____	_____	_____

Specific Gravity Temperature Correction		
Electrolyte Temperature		Adjusting Factor
°F	°C	
160	71.1	+.032
155	68.3	+.030
150	65.6	+.028
145	62.8	+.026
140	60.0	+.024
135	57.2	+.022
130	54.4	+.020
125	51.7	+.018
120	48.9	+.016
115	46.1	+.014
110	43.3	+.012
105	40.6	+.010
100	37.8	+.008
95	35.0	+.006
90	32.2	+.004
85	29.5	+.002
80	26.7	0.000
75	23.9	-.002
70	21.1	-.004
65	18.4	-.006
60	15.6	-.008
55	12.8	-.010
50	10.0	-.012
45	7.2	-.014
40	4.4	-.016
35	1.7	-.018
30	-1.1	-.020
25	-3.9	-.022
20	-6.7	-.024
15	-9.5	-.026
10	12.2	-.028

You may be able to spot a weak battery by its low voltage, but maybe not. Sometimes a battery will look fully charged at rest, but quickly lose its charge under load. A specific gravity test will reveal that problem.

Check the specific gravity of the electrolyte in each cell of each battery. This is a measurement of how concentrated the acid is in the battery, which also tells how fully charged it is. For both 6-volt and 12-volt batteries, the fully charged specific gravity should be about 1.265 per cell.

The instrument for checking specific gravity is a hydrometer. This is a large glass syringe with a calibrated glass float in it, and a rubber squeeze bulb at one end. It operates on the principle that the more concentrated the acid is (the higher the specific gravity), the higher the float will ride in it.

To use the hydrometer, insert the tip into the battery and squeeze the bulb to suck up electrolyte. You must pick up just enough to let the gauge inside float free—not resting on the bottom or bumping the top. To read the hydrometer, hold it so that the fluid is at your eye level, and read the number on the scale at that point, disregarding how the fluid curves up against the glass.

The temperature of the electrolyte will also affect its specific gravity. Batteries generate heat during charging, and hold that heat for a long time afterward. If you want to be really precise, you can use a thermometer to measure the temperature of the electrolyte, then adjust your specific gravity reading according to a temperature correction chart. An even easier method is to use a hydrometer with a built-in thermometer.

If you do replace a single battery, there is a technique for equalizing it to the rest of the pack. Put the new battery into its place in the pack, but wire around it, leaving it out of the circuit. Test the specific gravity of the electrolyte on the new battery with a hydrometer. Charge the rest of the pack until the specific gravity of the other batteries matches the new one. Then connect the new battery into the circuit and turn on the charger for the final equalizing finish charge.

Maintenance

Check tire pressure weekly, and adjust as needed. This is one of the most important maintenance items for good performance.

Check battery terminals for corrosion or loose connections once a month. Keep them clean and tight. Keep the battery tops clean as well. A thin film of dirt on the battery tops can form a conductive layer that will trip the ground fault interrupter on a charger.

Check battery electrolyte level and add water as needed every two months. If the plates are uncovered, add water to cover them by 1/8" before charging, and check the batteries more frequently in the future. Otherwise, add water after the batteries are charged. Fill each cell to 1/4" below the fill neck. Distilled water is preferred, but any drinkable water that does not have a high mineral content will do. Don't use metal containers for your battery water.

Testing specific gravity with a
hydrometer.

Check the brakes every six months, at least until
you learn how fast they are wearing. If you drive primarily on flat roads, and adjust your driving style to a
smooth flow that takes advantage of coasting, you may
find you actually use your brakes less.

This seems like a really short chapter, doesn't it?
Well, there just isn't much maintenance to do on an
electric car.

15

POSITIVE VS. NEGATIVE EV FACTS

Here are just a few examples of ways to answer the most common questions in a positive way. Think up your own positive answers to questions, and have them ready when people ask.

Range
Negative: Electric cars have short ranges. The average is only 60 - 80 miles, and some of the poorer ones get only 30 miles. Only a few of the best can get even 100 miles.
Positive: Ninety percent of the cars in America travel less than 25 miles a day, and even the worst electrics can do that. Most well-made modern conversions can do two or three times that, and the high-performance cars can do 100 miles or more.

Speed
Negative: Electric cars aren't as fast as gas cars.
Positive: Most well-made modern conversions can reach top speeds of 50 - 60 mph, and the high performance cars can get up to 80 - 90 mph.

Charging
Negative: Electric cars are inconvenient to refuel, because you can't just pull up to a corner gas station. Also, they take a long time to charge—as much as twelve hours.
Positive: Electric cars are easy to charge. Just plug into a regular 110-volt outlet. Most people don't use up a full charge in a day. Instead of finding a gas station, waiting in line, and wrestling with a smelly pump, you simply plug in at home at night, and the car is ready in the morning. Many

Meeting the Press

One of the first things you will discover as an EV owner is that an electric car is an instant ticket to local fame. You will find yourself stopped by strangers in parking lots, speaking to the Rotary Club, driving politicians in parades, and invited to participate in the Concours d' Elegance. You will also find yourself talking to reporters.

One of the next things you will discover is that the story the reporter files usually isn't nearly as enthusiastic about EVs as you are. In fact, the more important the venue for the story, the more likely that it will come out downright negative. "Electric cars can't. . . not yet. . .still limited. . ."

Knowing that you are an ambassador for EVs, and facing a skeptical world, here are some things you can do to improve the results.

Choose Your Forum
Not all publicity is good. If you are invited to participate in an eighty mile 'Clean Air Race' as the only electric among a pack of methanol and CNG cars, and you know you will limp in dead last if at all, don't go 'just to show the flag'. The flag doesn't show well dragging in the dust. Don't participate in events which you know will make your car look bad by comparison.

Prepare Your Car
Even club rallies, which are events within the EV 'family', attract a lot of general public and some media. Be sure your car is as clean and professional looking as you can possibly make it. If the paint is old, there are products to buff it up. At least wash and vacuum it. Clean the battery terminals. Take a few minutes to tie wrap wires tidily out of the way.

Above all, do not give rides to reporters if your car is not fully charged, or not up to snuff for any other reason. Too often, major media have ridden in undercharged or ailing cars and written about their pathetic performance. Don't give them another opportunity.

Accentuate The Positive
As they say, nobody notices planes that land safely, only the ones that crash. Likewise, nobody notices all the miles of reliable EV driving, only the one time you walked home. Even among ourselves, problems stick in our minds.

The media and general public already have negatives about EVs in their heads: EVs are small, weird-looking, slow, have short ranges, and are likely to run out of juice and leave you stranded. Don't feed these stereotypes. Before you open your mouth, remember the doctor's principle: first, do no harm.

Don't tell the reporter about the time you goofed

people drive ten or so miles to work, plug in all day, and have a full charge when they leave.

Running Out Of Electricity

Negative: What happens if you run out of juice before you get home? Most electric car owners have tow bars for rescues.
Positive: When a gas car runs out of gas, it stops dead, right now. An electric will simply start to slow down gradually over a period of several miles. If you finally must pull off the road, you can park for ten minutes, and the batteries will regain some charge just by resting. You can then drive a couple more miles, and rest again if need be. Try that with an empty gas tank!

Long Trips

Negative: You can't take long trips in an electric car.
Positive: An electric car is not intended for long trips, just as a microwave oven is not intended for frying foods or baking angel food cakes. Most people who have a microwave also have a conventional oven. Most households in America have more than one car. For long trips, take the other car.

Cost

Negative: It's expensive to buy or convert a car, and to replace the batteries when they need it.
Positive: An electric car is very cheap to operate. Even including replacing the batteries every three to four years, it still costs only about a third as much as a gas car. That's because there are no tune-ups, oil changes, mufflers, starters, water pumps, radiators, etc. And how do you place a dollar value on all the time you save not taking the car to the shop?

and had to walk home. Don't tell them how much extra effort you take to plan your routes carefully. (Is it really that much more effort?) Don't tell them you worry about having enough juice. These are the things they will blow up into headlines.

There are only about a dozen questions that everyone asks, but the same facts can be given in different ways, with different results. Is the glass half full, or half empty? Practice answers that are stated in a positive way. No sentence should start out, "An electric car can't. . ." or "With an electric car, you have to. . ."

Emphasize 'Normal'

If your car is a Citicar, or a home-built chassis, or a souped up race car with batteries everywhere, be sure the media and the public know that this is an unusual car. If possible, try to have a friend with a very ordinary-looking electric sedan included in the interview. The world in general already knows electric cars can be weird. Most of the world is put off by weird. They need to know electrics can be normal, too.

Give Information Bites

Reporters are looking for brief, clear quotes to use. Have some of your favorites ready. A single clear sentence will be quoted, maybe even highlighted. A lengthy discourse of run-on sentences will be condensed and edited by the reporter, if used at all. Any time the reporter edits you, your statements get farther from what you intended to say. Practice a few snappy quotes.

Have Printed Handouts

Send them away with something in writing they can refer to later. Always keep literature in your car, for surprise interviews in parking lots. You can get brochures from the Electric Auto Association, or "EV Fact Sheets" from Electro Automotive, or you can type up and copy a page of info about your own car.

When talking to the public or press, try to get inside the head of your audience. Try to dissolve their fears and surprise them with positive facts that will get them excited. Listen to what you're saying from their perspective, and see if it sounds positive or negative. Don't dwell on ideas of limits or handicaps, or anything that implies that people will have to make major sacrifices in their lives to own an electric.

We are all missionaries for electrics in a world of petroleum pagans. A sermon of joy is going to make more converts than one of chastity, poverty, and obedience. So go forth and preach the gospel!

Index

Illustrations in **bold face**.

<h1>The Most Complete Kits Available Anywhere</h1>
<h1>DC CONVERSION KITS FROM ELECTRO AUTOMOTIVE</h1>

Most of these components are also available separately. However, it is more economical to buy them in the kit package.

DELUXE UNIVERSAL KIT $6,425.00

This is a universal kit for converting small manual transmission gas or diesel vehicles to electricity. The adaptor is custom-machined to suit the transmission. All other model-specific parts (motor mounts, brackets, battery racks, etc.) must be designed and fabricated by the builder. The included manual gives guidelines for these items.

INCLUDES:

* WarP 9 Motor
* Adaptor
* Albright Main Contactor
* PMC-1221C Controller
* PB-6 Potbox
* Airpax Circuit Breaker
* Fusible Links

* Westach Gauge: 0-400 Amps
* Westach Gauge: 6-16 Volts
* Westach Gauge, Choice Of:
  Battery Pack Voltage Gauge, Or
  0-100% State-Of-Charge
* Empro Shunt
* DC/DC Converter

* 110VAC Zivan NG3 Charger
* 2/0 Fine Strand Cable
* Lugs
* Belleville Precision Tension
  Washers
* Shrink Tube
* Anti-Corrosion Compound

* Cable/Lug Crimper
* Cable Shears
* Digital Multimeter
* "Convert It" Manual

VOLTSRABBIT CUSTOM KIT $9,995.00 Sedan $10,085.00 Cabriolet/Convertible

This is the first true bolt-in kit: no design, fabrication, or welding necessary. **Fits all manual transmission Rabbits ('74-'84), and Cabriolets through '93. Seats four with cargo space. Can be easily modified to fit Rabbit pickup, Scirocco, or early Jettas Will NOT fit Golf, Cabrio, or Fox, or any other makes or models.** Features epoxy powder-coated battery racks and welded polypropylene battery box for acid resistance and electrical insulation. A 96 volt system gives a top speed of 65 mph and a range of 60-80 miles under optimum conditions. 108V option adds 2 batteries under back seat for 75 mph top speed and an extra 10% range. Can be installed in as little as four days. **This kit requires US Battery brand, model #US-125 6V golf cart batteries with "L" posts. No substitutions.**

INCLUDES:

* ImPulse 9 Motor
* Adaptor
* Albright Main Contactor
* PMC-1221C Controller
* PB-6 Potbox
* Airpax Circuit Breaker
* Fusible Links
* Empro Shunt
* Westach Gauge: 0-400 Amps

* Westach Gauge: 96 Volt
  State-Of-Charge
* 110VAC Russco Charger
* Power Brake Vacuum System
* Grill & Starter Blockoffs
* DC/DC Converter
* Battery Racks & Holddowns
* Battery Box & Vent Fan
* 2/0 Fine Strand Cable

* Lugs
* Copper Strap Battery Interconnects
* Belleville Precision Tension
  Washers
* Shrink Tube
* Anti-Corrosion Compound
* Cable/Lug Crimper
* Heavy-Duty Springs & Shocks
* Wiring Loom

* All Nuts, Bolts, & Hardware
* All Mounts & Brackets
* Cable Shears
* Special Tools & Supplies
* "Convert It" Manual
* Installation Instructions

VOLTSPORSCHE DC CUSTOM KIT $12,545.00

Like the Voltsrabbit, this is a completely pre-fabricated bolt-in kit. **Fits all manual transmission 4-cylinder Porsche 914s – NO other makes or models.** Features the same epoxy powder-coated battery racks and welded polypropylene battery boxes, plus a large motor and 120 volt system for 85 mph top speed and 80-100 miles range under optimum conditions. The rear trunk still has usable cargo space, and will accept the targa top. Can be installed in as little as six days. **This kit requires US Battery brand, model #US-125 6V golf cart batteries with "L" posts. No substitutions.**

INCLUDES:

* WarP 9 Motor
* Adaptor
* Albright Main Contactor
* PMC-1231C Controller
* PB-6 Potbox
* Airpax Circuit Breaker
* Fusible Links
* Westach Gauge: 0-500 Amps
* Westach Gauge: 50-150 Volts

* Empro Shunt
* 110 VAC Zivan NG3 Charger
* Starter Blockoff
* DC/DC Converter
* Battery Racks & Holddowns
* Battery Boxes & Vent Fans
* Heavy-Duty Springs, Torsion Bars,
  & Shocks
* All Mounts & Brackets

* Wiring Loom
* All Nuts, Bolts, & Hardware
* 2/0 Fine Strand Cable
* Lugs
* Copper Strap Battery Interconnects
* Belleville Precision Tension
  Washers
* Shrink Tube
* Anti-Corrosion Compound

* Cable/Lug Crimper
* Cable Shears
* Special Tools & Supplies
* Installation Instructions
* "Convert It" Manual

SUBSTITUTIONS & OPTIONS

Other motors, controllers, and chargers can be substituted in the kits at an adjusted price. Some components cannot be substituted in the custom Voltsrabbit and Voltsporsche kits due to physical space constraints.

Electro Automotive
POB 1113, Felton, CA 95018
Phone: (831) 429-1989 * Fax: (831) 429-1907
Email: electro@cruzio.com * Web Site: http://www.electroauto.com

The Most Complete Kits Available Anywhere
AC CONVERSION KITS FROM ELECTRO AUTOMOTIVE

AC systems offer the benefits of increased efficiency, regenerative braking, and the option of direct drive. Most of these components are also available separately. However, it is more economical to buy them in the kit package. All parts carry a 1 year warranty.

Voltsporsche AC Custom Kit - $14,635.00

This is an AC version of our popular DC Voltsporsche Kit. **It fits all manual transmission 4-cylinder Porsche 914 – NO other makes or models.** It uses the same battery racks & boxes and overall layout, but runs on a 144V pack of 8V batteries instead of 120V of 6V batteries. This car can reach a top speed of 100 mph and a range of 150 miles under good conditions. The ultimate combination of performance, range, and affordability. **This kit requires US Battery brand model #US8CVGC 8V golf cart batteries with "L" terminals, or Deka Dominator Group 24 12V gel batteries with "L" terminals. No substitutions.**

INCLUDES:
* Solectria AC24 Motor
* Adaptor
* Solectria DMOC445 Controller & Wiring Interface Kit
* PB-8 Potbox
* Fusible Links

*3 Westach Gauges & Shunt
* Zivan NG3 110VAC Charger w/ extension cord & AC inlet
* Starter Blockoff
* DC/DC Converter
* Battery Racks & Holddowns
* Battery Boxes & Ventilation

* Heavy-Duty Springs, Torsion Bars, & Shocks
* All Mounts & Brackets
* All Nuts, Bolts, & Hardware
* Cable, Lugs, Shrink Tube, Noalox, & Belleville Washers

* Battery Interconnects
* Special Tools
* Synthetic Trans Fluid
* Installation Instructions
* "Convert It" Manual

Universal Kits

The following kits are "universal" kits in the sense that they are not designed for any specific model of vehicle. They contain the drive components that are common to any conversion. It is left to the installer to design and fabricate the pieces that will customize the kit to his or her chassis. "Light Vehicle" kits are suitable for vehicles with factory curb weights (not gross vehicle weights) under 2,400 lbs. and require 144V. "Heavy Vehicle" kits are suitable for vehicles with factory curb weights between 2,400 and 3,500 lbs. and require 288V minimum, 321V recommended.

Light Vehicle Manual Transmission Kit - $9,435.00

This kit mounts the motor to the car's original manual transmission. The one custom piece that is included is the motor/transmission adaptor. We have a substantial library of adaptor patterns, and often an adaptor for one model of car will cross over to another model that you might not expect. If we do not have a pattern for your transmission, we can make one easily. Suitable for compacts, sports cars, and kit cars up to 2,400 lbs. original curb weight.

INCLUDES:
* Solectria AC24 Motor
* Adaptor
* PB-8 Potbox

* Solectria DMOC445 Controller & Wiring Interface Kit
* 3 Westach Gauges & Shunt
* DC/DC Converter

* Zivan NG3 110VAC Charger
* Cable, Lugs, Shrink Tube, Noalox, & Belleville Washers

* Special Tools
* Installation Instructions

Light Vehicle Direct Drive Kit - $11,090.00

This kit eliminates the transmission for smooth driving without shifting gears on front engine/front wheel drive vehicles. The kit includes Solectria gearbox and halfshafts with inner CV joints. You will need to take the halfshafts to an axle shop to cut to the appropriate length and fit with appropriate outer CV joints for your chassis. Suitable for compacts, sports cars, and kit cars up to 2,400 lbs. original curb weight.

INCLUDES:
* Solectria AC24 Motor
* Solectria DMOC445 Controller & Wiring Interface Kit

* PB-8 Potbox
* Zivan NG3 Charger
* Solectria AT1200 Gearbox, Supports, & Halfshafts,

* DC/DC Converter
* 3 Westach Gauges & Shunt
* Cable, Lugs & Belleville Precision Tension Washers

* Special Tools

Heavy Vehicle Manual Transmission Kit - $11,855.00

This kit mounts the motor to the car's original manual transmission. The one custom piece that is included is the motor/transmission adaptor. We have a substantial library of adaptor patterns, and often an adaptor for one model of car will cross over to another model that you might not expect. If we do not have a pattern for your transmission, we can make one easily. Suitable for mid-size sedans, pickup trucks, SUVs, and minivans up to 3,500 lbs. original curb weight.

INCLUDES:
* Solectria AC55 Motor
* Adaptor
* DC/DC Converter

* Solectria DMOC445 Controller & Wiring Interface Kit
*PB-8 Potbox

* Vacuum Power Brake System
* Zivan NG5 220VAC Charger
* 3 Westach Gauges & Shunt

* Cable, Lugs & Belleville Precision Tension Washers
* Special Tools

Electro Automotive
POB 1113, Felton, CA 95018
Phone: (831) 429-1989 * Fax: (831) 429-1907
Email: electro@cruzio.com * Web Site: http://www.electroauto.com